States of danger and deceit

Manchester University Press

States of danger and deceit

The European political thriller in the 1970s

Edited by

Rachel Hayward, Ellen Smith
and Andy Willis
A HOME Film Dossier

Manchester University Press

Copyright © Manchester University Press 2024

While copyright in the volume as a whole is vested in Manchester University Press, copyright in individual chapters belongs to their respective authors, and no chapter may be reproduced wholly or in part without the express permission in writing of both author and publisher.

Published by Manchester University Press
Oxford Road, Manchester M13 9PL

www.manchesteruniversitypress.co.uk

British Library Cataloguing-in-Publication Data
A catalogue record for this book is available from the British Library

Publication was supported by the BFI, awarding National Lottery funding

ISBN 978 1 5261 7643 1 hardback
ISBN 978 1 5261 7644 8 paperback

First published 2024

The publisher has no responsibility for the persistence or accuracy of URLs for any external or third-party internet websites referred to in this book, and does not guarantee that any content on such websites is, or will remain, accurate or appropriate.

Typeset by Newgen Publishing UK

Contents

List of figures	vii
Notes on contributors	viii
Acknowledgements	xi
Introduction – Rachel Hayward, Ellen Smith and Andy Willis	1
1 Creating a major film season at HOME: Reflections on putting together *States of Danger and Deceit: The European Political Thriller in the 1970s* – Andy Willis	4
2 France, May '68 and the development of the political thriller – Andy Willis	19
3 Costa-Gavras, Jorge Semprún and Yves Montand: Creating a model for a 'commercial' political cinema – Andy Willis	30
4 *State of Siege (État de siège)*, Costa-Gavras, 1973 – Andy Willis	39
5 *L'Attentat (Plot)*, Yves Boisset, 1972 – Andy Willis	49
6 *Special Section (Section spéciale)*, Costa-Gavras, 1975 – Rachel Hayward	59
7 The political thriller in the context of Italian cinema – Andy Willis	71
8 *Investigation of a Citizen above Suspicion (Indagine su un cittadino al di sopra di ogni sospetto)*, Elio Petri, 1970 – Ellen Smith	83
9 *Killer Cop (La polizia ha le mani legate)*, Luciano Ercoli, 1975 – MaoHui Deng	92

10	West Germany: Terrorism on the doorstep – Andy Willis	100
11	Neither intentional nor accidental, but unavoidable: *The Lost Honour of Katharina Blum* – Jason Wood	109
12	Where the political thriller was less prevalent – Andy Willis	118
13	*Operación Ogro* (*Ogro*), Gillo Pontecorvo, 1979 – Fraser Elliott	127
14	*Die Flucht* (*The Flight*), Roland Gräf, 1977 – Declan Clarke	136
15	*Days of '36* (*Meres tou '36*), Theo Angelopoulos, 1972 – Eleftheria Rania Kosmidou	148
16	Who is the man on the roof? – Roy Stafford	157
17	The legacy of the 1970s European political thriller – Andy Willis	167
18	The season: Films screened as part of *States of Danger and Deceit* – Rachel Hayward, Ellen Smith and Andy Willis	178
Index		190

Figures

1	*Investigation of a Citizen above Suspicion* (1970), courtesy of Park Circus/Criterion	1
2	*Illustrious Corpses* (1976), courtesy of Cristaldi Film	4
3	*Z* (1969), courtesy of KG Productions	19
4	*State of Siege* (1973), courtesy of KG Productions	30
5	*State of Siege* (1973), courtesy of KG Productions	39
6	Advertising poster for *L'Attentat* (1972)	50
7	*Special Section* (1975), courtesy of The Festival Agency (Paris)	59
8	*Don't Torture a Duckling* (1972), courtesy of Arrow Films	71
9	*Investigation of a Citizen above Suspicion* (1970), courtesy of Park Circus/Criterion	83
10	*Killer Cop* (1975), courtesy of Raro Video	92
11	*Knife in the Head* (1978), courtesy of StudioCanal Germany	100
12	*The Lost Honour of Katharina Blum* (1975), courtesy of StudioCanal	109
13	*Siete días de enero* (1979), courtesy of Mercury Video	118
14	*Operación Ogro* (1979), courtesy of Cristaldi Film	127
15	*Die Flucht* (1977), courtesy of Berlin DEFA Foundation	136
16	*Days of '36* (1972), courtesy of Artificial Eye	148
17	Advertising poster for *Man on the Roof* (1976), courtesy of Svenska Film Institut	157
18	*New Order* (2020), courtesy of MUBI	167
19	Season brochure cover, courtesy of HOME, Manchester	179

Contributors

Declan Clarke is an artist and filmmaker. His films have been shown internationally, screened at film festivals such as FIDMarseille, Tromsø International Film Festival and the New York Underground Film Festival and distributed in the UK by Curzon. He has exhibited internationally as an artist in institutions such as PS1 MoMA, New York; Tate Britain, London; HKW, Berlin; the Beijing Imperial City Art Museum; the 2nd Moscow Biennial; and the Centre for Contemporary Art, Lagos. In 2015, he was awarded the Jury Prize at the 31st Biennal of Graphic Arts, Ljubljana.

MaoHui Deng is a lecturer in Film Studies at the University of Manchester. His research is interested in the ways in which films about dementia and ageing can help further as well as complicate our understanding of time in cinema, gerontology and wider society. He is the author of *Ageing, Dementia and Time in Film: Temporal Performances* (Edinburgh University Press, 2023), and has published in the edited collections *Contemporary Narratives of Ageing, Illness, Care* (Routledge, 2022) and *The Politics of Dementia* (De Gruyter, 2022).

Fraser Elliott is a lecturer in Film, Exhibition and Curation at the University of Edinburgh. Prior to this appointment, he was a member of the Film team at HOME, Manchester, where he assisted in the delivery of the *States of Danger and Deceit* season in 2017. Alongside university work, he is involved in the programming and curation of Chinese-language cinema across Manchester and Edinburgh as a member of the Chinese Film Forum UK and is a collaborator with organisations including the Taiwan Film Festival Edinburgh.

Rachel Hayward is the Head of Film Strategy at HOME, Manchester. She is the director of the ¡*Viva! Spanish and Latin American Festival*, co-curator of *Not Just Bollywood* and a founder member of the Chinese Film Forum UK.

Eleftheria Rania Kosmidou is a lecturer in Film Production at the University of Salford. In her work, Rania studies European civil war films, cultural memory, Brechtian cinema and cinematic modernisms, the cinema of Theo Angelopoulos and weird contemporary Greek cinema. She has published on the above subjects in journals, edited collections and in her monograph *European Civil War Films: Memory, Conflict and Nostalgia* (Routledge, 2013; 2016). Rania has served as the guest editor of the special issue 'Studies in Cultural Memory' for the *Journal of Media and Cultural Politics* (Intellect, 2016).

Ellen Smith is a freelance film writer and worked as a project assistant on the *States of Danger and Deceit* film season at HOME in 2017.

Roy Stafford is a freelance lecturer and writer based in West Yorkshire. He has a long history of cinema-based film education activities for full-time students and public audiences. He feels privileged to have worked with Cornerhouse and HOME since the mid-1990s on a wide range of events. Having written teaching materials and textbooks for film and media studies for many years, Roy now blogs regularly about global film at itpworld.wordpress.com.

Andy Willis is Professor of Film Studies at the University of Salford. He is also, since 2015, Senior Visiting Curator for Film at HOME, Manchester. Most recently, he has been the co-editor of *DVD, Blu-ray and Beyond: Navigating Formats and Platforms within Media Consumption* (Palgrave, 2017) and *Cult Media: Re-Packaged, Re-Released and Restored* (Palgrave, 2017) with Jonathan Wroot, and *Chinese Cinemas: International Perspectives* (Routledge, 2016) with Felicia Chan.

Jason Wood is the Executive Director of Public Programmes and Audiences at the BFI. The author of multiple published works on cinema, he is also a contributor to *The Wire* and the co-curator of *Café Exil: New Adventures in European Music 1972–1980* for Ace Records.

Acknowledgements

States of Danger and Deceit: The European Political Thriller in the 1970s began life as a major season of films at HOME in Manchester and a subsequent UK tour, both of which formed part of the BFI's Thriller season in autumn/winter 2017. Jessie Gibbs was the Coordinator of the HOME season and tour, and we would like to thank her for all her work. We would also like to thank all the programmers at UK venues who took the season, presented accompanying events and helped make it such a success. At HOME, we would like to acknowledge the support of Jason Wood, Jen Hall, the technical and projection teams, and the many staff who provided valuable support. Thanks also to Isabelle Croissant for her guidance on some translations in this collection. The University of Salford also supported Andy Willis's secondment to HOME during the period that covered the season, and Martin Flanagan and Pete Deakin proved once again to be supportive Film Studies colleagues in this regard. We would also like to thank Matthew Frost at Manchester University Press for his support for this dossier-style publication as well as all the contributors for writing their chapters in a fashion that acknowledged this. The cover was designed by Trish Brennan for the season's poster. Images within the volume are those used to promote the *States of Danger and Deceit* screenings, and as this volume rounds off the events of the season, they are used in the spirit of advertising. The season and this publication were supported by the BFI, awarding National Lottery funding.

Introduction

Rachel Hayward, Ellen Smith and Andy Willis

Figure 1 *Investigation of a Citizen above Suspicion* (1970), courtesy of Park Circus/Criterion

The *States of Danger and Deceit: The European Political Thriller in the 1970s* dossier is a key component of a project that took place at HOME in Manchester and across the UK in late 2017 and early 2018. HOME, a major arts centre in Manchester, England, opened in 2015. At its core, it consists of two theatres, two gallery spaces and five cinema screens. As an independent cinema, it is responsible for creating its own programme and, as part of that, has created a number of retrospectives and themed seasons. *States of Danger and Deceit* was one of these. The season and tour were developed and delivered by a core team of three based at HOME: Andy Willis (Curator), Rachel Hayward (Producer) and Jessie Gibbs (Coordinator). The impetus for such a large-scale series of events was provided by the model established by HOME's earlier large-scale film season *CRIME: Hong Kong Style*, which had been delivered by the same team and took place in Manchester and on tour across the UK between February and April 2016. At the core of *States of Danger and Deceit* was a film season that brought together a range of work that in some way related to the idea of the European political thriller film and its particular manifestation in Europe in the 1970s. A list of the films that made up the season can be found at the end of this volume whilst the rationale behind the season is explored in the following chapter.

From the outset, this HOME film dossier was envisaged as a key part of the legacy of the *States of Danger and Deceit* project. In order to remain true to the spirit of the season, it was decided early on that it would include a number of those who had contributed introductions and programme notes, and offered longer one-hour presentations as part of the programme. Central to this was a commitment to draw on new voices alongside more established writers who had a history of collaboration with HOME. We are confident that this combination has resulted in a variety of insightful engagements with a number of the political thrillers produced in Europe during the 1970s.

Our aim in putting together a HOME film dossier was to provide a range of informed and accessible primer pieces. In order to achieve this, we have a number of contextualising chapters that are followed by considerations of key individual films, most of which were screened as part of HOME's season. The most coverage is given to films produced within the context of the French film industry. This is due to both the number of relevant films made in France and the political upheavals that were heralded by the events in Paris during May 1968. In addition, the work of director Costa-Gavras and his collaborators and imitators is widely regarded as the model for the political thriller in Europe. The one contribution that does not focus on a film screened in Manchester is *L'Attentat* (*Plot*), a 1972 French–Italian co-production that is included to ensure that the French section does not over-simplistically just focus on the work of Costa-Gavras. This section of the dossier is followed by a focus on Italy, another highly productive film industry that offered a wide range of political engagements with the form of the thriller. The next section focuses on West Germany. Whilst the sheer number of films produced there is significantly less than in France and Italy, the political context is still one of the most emblematic of the decade, incorporating as it does groups such as the Red Army Faction (*Rote Armee Fraktion*), commonly referred to as the Baader-Meinhof Group. The next contributions offer a more wide-ranging exploration of films and countries where the political thriller was less common. These include East Germany, Greece, Spain and Sweden. The inclusion of these ensures that this dossier does not simply focus on the dominant industries of the period but offers a wide-ranging exploration of the idea of the political thriller across Europe in the 1970s. Throughout, we have used English language titles alongside the original where they are in common use. When the original title is the most familiar, we have used that and offered an English translation where appropriate.

For those returning to the form of the European political thriller, we hope our contributors offer something that inspires a revisiting of some of these landmark films, produced during a particularly politically complex decade. For those readers new to the European political thriller, we hope that what follows goes some way to encouraging you to seek out these somewhat overlooked cinematic gems. If you do, we are sure you will not be disappointed.

1

Creating a major film season at HOME: Reflections on putting together *States of Danger and Deceit: The European Political Thriller in the 1970s*

Andy Willis

Figure 2 *Illustrious Corpses* (1976), courtesy of Cristaldi Film

Creating a major film season such as *States of Danger and Deceit* is a major undertaking. This can be broken down into three distinct components: firstly, researching possible titles for the season and engaging with the critical writing about the form of the political thriller in Europe; secondly, the selection of the films and the designing of supporting events and materials; and finally, the actual delivery of the season. In this part of the dossier, I will outline these three areas, offering some thoughts and reflections on the process which represents a clear combination of research and practice. This approach is something that has been developed at HOME, and its previous incarnation Cornerhouse, through the major film seasons that took place in Manchester and on tour across the UK: *Visible Secrets: Hong Kong's Women Filmmakers* (co-curated by Sarah Perks and Andy Willis in 2009) and *CRIME: Hong Kong Style* (curated by Andy Willis in 2016).

Contexts: issues of definition

Films that set about tackling political themes and offering tales set amongst the political classes were not new in the late 1960s and early 1970s. There had been notable Hollywood examples of what might be considered 'political thrillers' earlier in the 1960s such as *The Manchurian Candidate* (John Frankenheimer, 1962), which explored the idea of Cold War brainwashing, and *Seven Days in May* (John Frankenheimer, 1964), which imagined a military plot to overthrow the US government. Both of these examples articulated ideas about a lack of trust of the establishment that were beginning to coalesce within American society at the time. Globally, the late 1960s was a period of increased social turmoil which saw the emergence of newly politicised social groups and created an environment where political films would find an attentive and enthusiastic audience. Politics had become hot news and political activism seemed to be all around on university campuses, in the factories and on the streets. Filmgoers who had been politicised by key historical events of the 1960s increasingly found they could no longer say nothing about France's colonial war in Algeria, the USA and its allies' escalating involvement in Vietnam and, as the decade drew to a close, the student uprisings in Paris widely referred to as May '68 and the

Soviet Union's repressive military intervention in Czechoslovakia's Prague Spring of the same year. Filmmakers, some out of political commitment, others out of commercial opportunism, were more than happy to provide works that explored these contemporary issues and spoke to audiences' concerns. At the forefront of this shift were the Hollywood conspiracy thriller and the European political thriller.

Issues of simple and straightforward definitions are always difficult when it comes to film genres, and this is perhaps more so when it comes to the thriller. This had led to those writing about particular trends or cycles within the broad thriller label focusing on the narrowing, defining feature. For example, when writing about the erotic thriller, Linda Ruth Williams chooses to offer a sophisticated exploration of the erotic part of the term as its defining characteristic (2005: 17–21). A useful working definition of the term thriller is offered by Christopher Wicking when he argues that 'the touchstone of the thriller is tension'. He goes on to acknowledge the difficulty in tying down the idea of a film thriller, stating:

> There are also more variations to the thriller than any other of the genres ... There's the gangster thriller, the psychological thriller, the chase thriller, the 'in the streets' thriller, the comedy thriller, the detective thriller and so on – few films fitting simply into one or other category but many with overlapping characteristics, while the genre as a whole shares several stylistic trappings with horror.
>
> 2005: 220

When it comes to thinking about the political thriller, there are once again various approaches to the body of work that may be given the label. It is therefore appropriate to take Wicking's touchstone of tension and then consider the contexts within which that tautness is generated. When the filmmakers have used particular political and social situations to generate the required tension, there is the making of a political thriller. What the politics, in terms of left and right, may be is something that can be extrapolated through critical analysis.

Today, when one thinks of the political thrillers of the 1970s, many turn to those produced in Hollywood. However, that era of thriller production within the mainstream US film industry is also identified by Michael Ryan and Douglas Kellner as containing a number of films that they argue are representative of a new conservatism within the USA. As they put it: 'A meaner, more cynical discourse began to emerge as the dominant mode of Hollywood film. In 1971 alone, *The French Connection* [William Friedkin], *Dirty Harry* [Don Siegal], and *Straw Dogs* [Sam Peckinpah] articulate an antiliberal value system that portrays human life as predatory and animalistic, a jungle without altruism' (1988: 39). In this configuration, the thriller as a form is at the behest of right-wing ideas. As Ryan and Kellner articulate it, these 'law and order thrillers' reflect the discourse against crime and drugs being driven by the likes of Richard Nixon and Spiro Agnew in the early 1970s (1988: 41–42). Central to this was an attack on the liberal ideas that are widely seen as emblematic of America in the late 1960s.

The criticism of Hollywood thrillers offered by Ryan and Kellner is significant as it reminds us that film genres and styles such as the thriller are spaces of contestation and debate. The thriller itself is not inherently liberal or left wing; rather, it was a series of politically engaged filmmakers who, in the 1970s, used the raw material of the format to put forward their opinions. Indeed, Ryan and Kellner suggest this themselves when, later in their exploration of the politics of contemporary Hollywood cinema, they identify the political thriller as 'one of the primary arenas for liberal critiques of U.S. society' (1988: 95). The term they use is 'conspiracy thrillers', arguing that 'In liberal conspiracy films, large institutions like the CIA are depicted as being corrupt, and such representations ... appealed to populist distrust of big institutions and politicians' (1988: 97). Mike Wayne usefully links these liberal Hollywood films to their European precursors when he argues:

> Hollywood directors appropriated this form in such films as *The Parallax View* (Alan J. Pakula, 1974), *Three Days of the Condor* (Sydney Pollack, 1975) and *All the President's Men* (Alan J. Pakula, 1976). In some films it is the role of private corporations and big business which is the site of conspiracy; in others, it is the state, or a mixture of the two.
>
> 2001: 69

The left-liberal drive of these films and their use of a rather mainstream style that was not inherently 'political' led to a number of criticisms of the idea and form of the left-wing political thriller that have continued since the 1970s.

Contexts: the political thriller debate

Whilst director Costa-Gavras's work in the 1970s represents some of the highest achievements of the cycle of political thrillers produced in Europe, it also helped spark the post-'68 debate within film culture about how far a 'political' film can be effective if it utilises mainstream forms such as the thriller. Emblematic of these debates is the work of Jean-Luc Comolli and Paul Narboni, whose influential 1969 editorial in *Cahiers du Cinema*, reprinted in English in *Screen* in 1971, suggested that as well as having political content to be truly effective, political filmmakers needed to challenge on the level of form. In such discussions, the work of Costa-Gavras and that of other proponents of the political thriller such as Yves Boisset and Alan J. Pakula were seen as ultimately compromised politically due to their adopting the form of mainstream, and thus bourgeois, cinema.

These filmmakers and their approach to making political films were pitted intellectually against the formally more experimental work of the likes of post-'68 Jean-Luc Godard and particularly his work with the Dziga Vertov Collective such as the pseudo-western *Le Vent d'est* (*Wind from the East*, 1970). As well as boasting a script contribution from one of the leaders of the May '68 events, Daniel Cohn-Bendit, for *Le Vent d'est*, the Collective were also able to utilise the star presence of Italian actor Gian Maria Volonté. Closely associated with the Italian Communist Party, itself moving away from the orbit of influence of Moscow, Volonté appeared in numerous politically driven, but formally more mainstream, films by key left-wing directors in Italy such as Elio Petri and Francesco Rosi, both of whom made some of the best examples of the European political thriller in the 1970s.

The discussions around the effectiveness of the politics of the political thriller would become labelled 'the political thriller debate', and focused on how far mainstream conventional films could be considered as politically progressive. As John Hill put it, 'For supporters of political thrillers, their great strength was their ability to both excite and maintain the interest of an audience who would normally be turned off by politics', whereas in contrast:

> for their detractors, the weakness of such films was that their use of popular forms inevitably diluted or compromised their capacity to be genuinely politically radical and to stimulate active political thought.

From this point of view, radical political purposes were more likely to be bent to the ends of mainstream Hollywood than vice versa.

1991: 38

At the core of this kind of criticism of the political thriller was the idea that such accounts of highly political situations tended towards explanations that centred on individuals rather than wider social and economic factors. As we shall see through the various examples discussed in this volume, the struggle to place their characters in such wider social, political and economic contexts is one of the hurdles that a number of filmmakers are actively involved in through their creative process. As Hill points out, one of the ways that they overcame this was to focus on the idea of conspiracy, because:

> Conspiracy theory, in this respect, has the virtue of neatness but it is also at the expense of genuine social and political complexity. Conspiratorial actions can be dramatised in a way that underlying social and economic forces cannot within the conventions of narrative and realism and, hence, 'conspiracy' becomes the preferred form of 'explanation' for how power is exercised in society and how events are to be accounted for.
>
> 1991: 37–38

For whatever the strengths and weaknesses of the actual message which the political thriller succeeds in communicating, it is still one that is, so to speak, 'pre-digested'. That is to say, opponents of the political thriller have argued that by virtue of a reliance upon individual characters and 'stars' with whom we identify, and upon the tightly structured patterns of narrative suspense which engage us emotionally rather than intellectually, the political thriller 'makes up our minds for us' (Hill, 1991: 40).

However, as we shall see across this volume, when engaged about their practice, a number of filmmakers articulated their rationale for the strategy of making more commercially orientated political films such as thrillers. For example, Elio Petri states that he chooses to draw on a variety of popular forms in order to reach a wide audience with his ideas. In a 1972 interview, he said that these:

> are expressed in very simple, popular didactic terms. Cinema is not for an elite, but for the masses. The acting and use of the camera must be a spectacular one. We as well have to take into account

the rich, popular tradition which is the basis of the Italian theatre and cinema.

Petri, 1983: 58

These formal decisions, for Petri, involve drawing on approaches that are not in line with middle-brow ideas of good taste, in particular, the value of psychologically rounded characters. Rather, he argued against what he saw as a 'snobbish, intellectual cinema' that required 'understatement', noting that 'reality is caricature and I believe that cinema should stress this, even if it means resorting to very popular forms' (Petri, 1983: 58).

Why revisit political thrillers from Europe?

The political thriller debate reminds one that the European political thriller was central to discussions about politics and film in the 1970s and 1980s, particularly to those that asked 'can political issues be adequately represented in mainstream forms?' Since then, to a certain degree, both these debates and a number of the films that sparked them have faded from audience consciousness. This is something that is reflected by the wider lack of visibility of the type of film that made up the *States of of Danger and Deceit* season on UK independent cinema screens. A starting point for the development of the season was therefore the question: is this a deserved state of affairs given the world of politics today?

In order to address this question, the team behind the season were determined that *States of Danger and Deceit* would not simply be driven by nostalgia, offering aged filmgoers the opportunity to see some old films they liked and were already familiar with. Rather, it would present a programme that aimed to connect the issues and ideas raised by the set of films screened with some of the concerns of contemporary society and by extension cinema audiences. In particular, we envisaged a season of films that responded to the recent waves of interest in political issues and activism, especially amongst young people seeking to have an interaction with and influence on their world as it shifts and changes around them. The films and events that supported the season therefore contained a range of ideas, images and stories that we hoped would be seen as relevant to the first part of the twenty-first century. In particular, they intersected with a wide range of issues and concerns that we felt were very much alive and had been the focus of recent discussion and debate, such as:

- The power of political elites.
- Ideological division.
- Corruption/manipulation of state institutions.
- Government-/state-sanctioned violence.
- What are the limits of liberal democracy?
- Radicalisation and terrorism.
- What are legitimate methods of resistance?
- Managing and policing radical ideas.
- Western interventionism and neocolonialism.
- Gender and radical politics.

These issues could be distilled into more general questions and concerns, which the season actively sought to engage with audiences about. These included:

- What is democracy today?
- How can we understand populism and/through film?
- Questions of social control and representation.
- The relationship between radical politics and identity politics.
- Race, gender and class revisited.
- Regional identities.

Furthermore, and ensuring that the conceptualisation of the season never lost sight of the fact that it was focused on films, we also sought to raise significant questions that were more focused on practice. In particular, what lessons might be learned by today's filmmakers from European political thrillers of the 1970s when it comes to making socially conscious work? In addressing this array of concerns, we aimed to design a film season that offered space for issue-based discussions sparked by the content of the work screened alongside considerations of the questions about film form raised by the decisions made by filmmakers in the 1970s to engage audiences.

As noted, some of the films that had been so central to debates about politics and film in the 1970s and 1980s had slowly become less visible and were rarely screened in UK cinemas. This was brought into focus by the continued UK reissues of Jean-Luc Godard's political films of the late 1960s and early 1970s in various formats. For example, Arrow Films released *La Chinoise* (1967) and *Tout va bien*

(1972), made with Jean-Pierre Gorin and the Dziga Vertov Group, on Blu-ray in the UK in April 2018 and August 2017 respectively. Compared with these, the more commercial political thrillers of the same era were much more difficult to find. One of the initial drivers in the design of *States of Danger and Deceit* was therefore making available films that had not been in cinemas (or widely available on domestic formats) for some time. In doing this, we hoped to rekindle and widen the debates around form and political cinema which seemed highly relevant in the late 2010s.

Identifying key films and approaches

Whilst the season focused on political thrillers from across Europe, it was important to structure it around a number of recognisable elements that would help audiences navigate what was on offer. Foremost amongst this was the identification of key countries where the politics of the era was particularly fraught and the form of the thriller was prevalent. This led to a primary focus, reflected in this dossier, on films made in France and Italy. In addition, West Germany was another country where the era's politics had thrown up some iconic organisations, such as the Red Army Faction (*Rote Armee Fraktion*), whose presence on the political scene had inspired a number of debates and films that we wanted to engage with in the season.

The presence of certain directors and performers would also provide audiences with a starting point for entry to the season. Foremost of these was Costa-Gavras, whose films, such as *Z* (1969), *State of Siege* (*État de Siège*, 1972) and *Special Section* (*Section spéciale*, 1975), form the focus of the first part of this dossier. After moving to France from Greece, in the late 1960s and early 1970s, Costa-Gavras established himself at the forefront of political filmmaking, creating work that, rather than the formal experiments of the likes of Godard, utilised the more mainstream form of the thriller. These films are widely discussed as being the archetypal examples of the political thriller of this period.

In the context of Italy, a key filmmaker was Francesco Rosi. Following his debut work *Salvatore Giuliano* (1962) and the subsequent *Hands over the City* (*Le mani sulla* città, 1963), Rosi had established himself as one of the major directors of post-neorealist Italian cinema. By the 1970s, he was directing taut, political films that often explored political corruption and violence through the form of an investigation. These included *The Mattei Affair* (*Il Caso Mattei*, 1972), *Lucky Luciano* (1974) and *Illustrious Corpses* (*Cadaveri Eccellenti*, 1975), all of which we intended to screen as part of *States of Danger and Deceit*. However, due to rights issues, although we found a screenable print of *Lucky Luciano*, we were in the end unable to include it in the season.

Elio Petri was another Italian director who made political films that had commercial appeal whom we were determined to include in the season. He had made works in the late 1960s and early 1970s that were highly relevant but outside the 1970s political thriller remit of the season, such as *We Still Kill the Old Way* (*A ciascuno il suo*, 1967), *The Working Class Goes to Heaven* (*La classe operaia va in paradiso*, 1971) and *Todo modo* (*One Way or Another*, 1976). Whilst Rosi is perhaps much less well known today than he was in the 1970s and 1980s, making his films ripe for rediscovery in the context of a season of political thrillers from Europe, it is certainly possible to argue that this is even more the case regarding Petri's work of the period. For that reason, we chose to include *Investigation of a Citizen above Suspicion* (*Indagine su un cittadino al di sopra di ogni sospetto*, 1970), a high-profile Oscar winner in its day but now much less well remembered by UK audiences.

Another Italian director we initially thought should form a significant part of the season was Damiano Damiani. Best known outside Italy for his political western *Bullet for the General* (*Quién sabe?*, 1966), he had worked much more closely to the mainstream of Italian popular cinema for his series of late 1960s and 1970s political thrillers, and his work often focused on the fight against organised crime and police and judicial corruption. Like Rosi and Petri, he had also used the work of writer Leonardo Sciascia as source material, in particular, *Day of the Owl* (*Il giorno della civetta*, 1968), in which a police officer, played by Franco Nero, is sent to investigate the murder of a building supplier. What he discovers is a web of corruption and lies that takes in the judiciary, the police and even the Catholic Church. His other work of the period also explored the idea of corruption within the political institutions of Italy, for example, *Confessions of a Police*

Commisioner (*Confessione di un commissario di polizia al procuratore della repubblica*, 1971), *The Case Is Closed, Forget It* (*L'istruttoria è chiusa: dimentichi*, 1971) and *How to Kill a Judge* (*Perché si uccide un magistrato*, 1975). As a commercial filmmaker, Damiani worked repeatedly with a number of top Italian stars such as Nero and imported American character actors such as Lee J. Cobb and Martin Balsam. However, the more overtly commercial nature of Damiani's work meant that it was released internationally in dubbed rather than subtitled versions. In turn, that meant that it was much more difficult to find prints that were screenable as part of the season and, ultimately, we had to choose to not screen any of these important works. This was done in the hope that maybe at a later date we would come across a version that we could use in the context of a UK cinema, whose audiences often prefer to see what they perceive to be original-language versions of films.

In putting the final season together, we also had other issues with rights and print availability. For example, we could not source the rights for the Sam Fuller-directed, West German film *Dead Pigeon on Beethoven Street* (*Tote Taube in der Beethovenstraße*, 1972). Originally an episode of the iconic German television series *Tatort*, Fuller's film obliquely engaged with the European thriller with its tale of an American detective investigating the death of a friend and the blackmailing of prominent politicians. A restored feature-length version with music by Can exists but, in the end, we were unable to screen it. It was a similar story with the Irish-set *The Outsider* (Tony Luraschi), a 1980 adaptation of Colin Lenster's novel *The Heritage of Michael Flaherty* that starred Craig Wasson as a disillusioned Vietnam veteran who travels to Ireland to join the fight for the Republican cause. Although originally bearing the Paramount logo and recently released on domestic formats, it proved difficult to clear the rights and find a print we could use, so we had to omit this little-known title that would have likely intrigued audiences.

The final season

For such an extensive season, HOME was able to draw on a number of their regular collaborators to gain financial support for individual screenings and events. These included the *Alliance*

Creating a major film season at HOME 15

Française de Manchester (Costa-Gavras screenings), the Embassy of Sweden in London (*Man on the Roof*, Bo Widerberg, 1976) and the University of Salford. The support of the BFI, awarding funds from the National Lottery, was given to HOME to support the season, of which this publication was an output. When we first approached the BFI with the idea for the season, we were informed that, coincidentally, they were in the initial stages of planning a major national 'blockbuster' season on the thriller titled *Who Can You Trust?* This followed their previous larger-scale programming initiatives which had focused on science fiction films, horror and Black film stars. For the team at HOME, this was a fortuitous coincidence as we were invited to become part of the touring offer alongside another roster of thriller titles from the Independent Cinema Office (ICO). Cinemas who wanted to become part of *Who Can You Trust?* could therefore select a number of titles from the list offered by the ICO and that curated by HOME.

This support enabled a final programme of twenty screenings at HOME between 4 November and 12 December 2017. Details of the films that made the final season can be found at the end of this dossier, including some titles that were available to tour only as they had recently screened at HOME. It is worth noting here that in drawing together the final list of films, it was important to have some titles that audiences may have had some familiarity with in order to offer a gateway to the wider offer of the season. For this reason, we included titles that presented a suggestion of what sorts of films the season might offer. For example, the perennially popular UK–France co-production *Day of the Jackal* (Fred Zinnemann, 1973) was included alongside the more well-known Costa-Gavras and Rosi titles *Z* and *Illustrious Corpses*. The season opened with a screening of *Z*, which was both the earliest selection on offer and, for many, the model for the European political thriller of the 1970s.

As well as the familiar, and to ensure that the season also challenged simple definitions of what might constitute a European political thriller, titles such as *Twilight's Last Gleaming* (1977) were included. This example was directed by a Hollywood filmmaker, Robert Aldrich, and starred Hollywood actors Burt Lancaster and Richard Widmark, but was also partly financed with West German money and shot in Bavaria. Questions were asked by HOME audiences about the inclusion of the Italian film *Don't Torture a Duckling* (Lucio Fulci, 1972). Our response was that the *giallo* is a form of commercial thriller, the film's themes are clearly political and so it might well be considered as suitable for inclusion in a season of European political thrillers. What was most satisfying was the fact that its inclusion ignited a debate about both its content and form as well as asked questions about how one might define the European political thriller.

In addition to screening the season's films, a range of supporting materials was devised to encourage audience engagement with the themes and ideas of *States of Danger and Deceit*. Reflecting the positive feedback for the supporting materials that had been produced for HOME's previous large-scale retrospective season, 2016's *CRIME: Hong Kong Style* (see Elliott and Willis, 2020), these included programme notes on films and directors, podcasts, a season poster, a genre map and a short trailer. One of the most conventional styles of supporting events adopted was the one-hour introduction to the themes of the season, and this was offered at strategic points across the season before key screenings. Further information can be found at the end of this dossier. Another familiar format utilised during the season was a Q&A session with actor Angela Winkler following the screening of *The Lost Honour of Katherina Blum* (Volker Schlöndorff and Margarethe von Trotta, 1975) at HOME. As noted elsewhere in this dossier, Winkler was a key performer in West German films that addressed issues related to terrorism in the 1970s, so she proved to be an excellent guest. Whilst in Manchester, she also recorded an interview which other venues screening the film were able to access and which was posted on HOME's website. Feedback from the audience suggested that many were very pleased to be able to ask questions of such an iconic performer of the period.

Perhaps the most innovative of HOME's supporting events was the invitation to Declan Clarke (https://homemcr.org/person/declan-clarke/) to act as an artist-in-residence for the season. Berlin-based Clarke, whose artistic practice intersected with the themes of the season, visited HOME during the season and took part in a number of events including film introductions, post-screening discussions and reflective events, and he has also contributed to this dossier.

The construction of the season was also undertaken with a firm commitment to utilising the talents of young people. To this end, HOME also created two student placements to work on the season. Ellen Smith and Laura Turney, both studying film at the University of Salford, worked with the Film and Communications teams at HOME to gain valuable insights into how a large-scale season is created and delivered. Smith has contributed to this dossier as both a writer and editor. Young people also formed the core of a small programming group known as 'the team', which was established to input into the selection of one of HOME's screenings in the season. After some discussion, they were responsible for putting forward *Killer Cop* (Luciano Ercoli, 1975), which team member MaoHui Deng introduced when it screened at HOME and writes about in this dossier.

In addition, ten titles were made available to other UK cinemas as part of a nationwide tour, along with the range of supporting materials developed at HOME such as posters and the opportunity to fund speakers associated with the HOME events or who were local experts in the field. The support of the BFI meant that for smaller independents, special rental rates could be offered in order to encourage wider participation in the season. This led to twenty-five other venues taking part in the tour from November 2017 to January 2018 and selecting anything from one title (The Hive in Shrewsbury) to all ten (the Leeds Film Festival, using the city's Everyman and Hyde Park Picture House cinemas and Leeds Town Hall). Those UK venues that took part in the tour of *States of Danger and Deceit* were: ArtHouse, Crouch End; BFI Southbank; The Cube, Bristol; DCA, Dundee; Deptford Cinema, London; Eden Court, Inverness; Edinburgh Filmhouse; GFT, Glasgow; The Hive, Shrewsbury; Kinokulture, Oswestry; Leeds Everyman; Leeds Hyde Park Picture House; Leeds Town Hall; Lewes Depot; MAC, Birmingham; Nottingham Broadway; Otley Film Society; Picturehouse at FACT, Liverpool; Quad, Derby; RBCFT, Dumfries; Showroom, Sheffield; Stoke Film Theatre; Storyhouse, Chester; Tyneside Cinema; and Watershed, Bristol.

The fact that *States of Danger of Deceit* was picked up by so many venues suggests that programmers across the country also felt that the titles we identified as significant and thought-provoking could in fact still connect with audiences. This was reflected when

I travelled to introduce *Investigation of a Citizen above Suspicion* to a packed house at The Hive in Shrewsbury and when I battled across the snow-covered Pennine hills to offer some thoughts about *The Lost Honour of Katherina Blum* to an enthusiastic crowd from the Otley Film Society at the local Courthouse arts centre.

References

Comolli, J.-L. and Narboni, P. (1971). 'Cinema/Ideology/Criticism'. *Screen*, 12(1), 27–38.

Elliott, F. and Willis, A. (2020). 'Rapidly Shifting Landscapes: Two Case Studies in the UK Distribution and Exhibition of Chinese Language Films in the Twenty-First Century'. In L. Feng and J. Aston (Eds), *Renegotiating Film Genres in East Asian Cinemas and Beyond*. London: Palgrave, 17–40.

Hill, J. (1991). '*Hidden Agenda*: Politics and the Thriller'. *Circa*, 57 (May–June), 36–41.

Petri, E. (1983). 'Cinema Is Not for the Elite, but for the Masses'. In D. Georgakas and L. Rubenstein (Eds), *The Cineaste Interviews: On Art and Politics of the Cinema*. Chicago: Lake View Press, 53–63.

Ryan, M. and Kellner, D. (1988). *Camera Politica: The Politics and Ideology of Contemporary Hollywood Film*. Bloomington: Indiana University Press.

Wayne, M. (2001). *Political Film: The Dialectics of Third Cinema*. London: Pluto Press.

Wicking, C. (1981). 'Thrillers'. In D. Pirie (Ed.), *Anatomy of the Movies*. London: Windward, 220–231.

Williams, L. R. (2005). *The Erotic Thriller in Contemporary Cinema*. Edinburgh: Edinburgh University Press.

2

France, May '68 and the development of the political thriller

Andy Willis

Figure 3 Z (1969), courtesy of KG Productions

A number of concerns that revolved around social issues involving social class, gender and race, as well as the post-colonial anger that was in the air and the protests against the US involvement in Vietnam, came to a head in the spring of 1968 in Paris. The build-up to May '68 had seen a number of protests, strikes and occupations. These impacted upon factories, university campuses and other institutions within France. The widespread upheavals and the anger that was driving them caused many within the ruling institutions of France to fear that civil war was a real possibility. The reality of this concern is clearly reflected in the fact that in late May, President De Gaulle left Paris for West Germany. The response to the protests from the police and other elements of the state apparatus was heavy-handed and led to violent clashes on the streets.

The events of May '68 had an enormous cultural impact and led to widespread discussion regarding the relationship between politics and culture. As Susan Hayward notes, they show France as 'a nation that was maturing politically, partly because modern technology meant that news travelled faster than ever before, but also because 1968 had been a watershed year for awareness, including an awareness about international politics' (2005: 265). In particular, she highlights the anti-Vietnam War movement and the women's movement as, crucially, further contributing to this growing awareness of political issues.

Raised amongst these critical debates were questions about the role of political filmmaking and which approaches to the medium were the most useful and effective politically. Reflecting on the period after May '68 in 1974, Guy Hennebelle usefully divided the post-1968 cinematic output in France into three tendencies. The first could be labelled as 'militant cinema' and involved films that sought to show the experiences of workers. The makers of such work often existed outside the professional film industry and operated in collectives and activist-based groups. Their work was often shot using semi-professional or amateur equipment such as 16mm film stock. The films themselves were often screened outside the usual avenues of distribution such as at workers' gatherings, activist meetings or community screenings. As Hennebelle put it, 'Ideologically-advanced film-makers, both professional and non-professional, realizing that it wasn't possible in our beautiful liberal democracy to make films on the social-economic-political reality began to work outside the established production-distribution system' (1974: 28).

The second tendency identified by Hennebelle is typified by the political filmmaking practice of the likes of Jean-Luc Godard and

Jean-Marie Straub. This work adopted a formally radical approach that drew on the work of practitioners such as Bertolt Brecht, and in particular his theories of distantiation in theatre practice, in order to create films that attempted to withdraw the emotional investment of audiences and replace it with a more thoughtful and ultimately politicised critical engagement with the representations on screen. Hennebelle, rather dismissively, describes this trend as 'incapable of answering concretely to the needs of the most politicized French viewers, drowning itself in formalism, intellectualism and ultraleftism' (1974: 29).

The third trend, which Hennebelle described as ' "cinema of the Z series" or Z movies' (1974: 29) after Costa-Gavras's 1969 release Z, is the political thriller. He goes on, rather critically, to argue that these Z movies reflect the standardising influence of American filmmaking styles on international popular cinema and that they represent an acceptance of the formula of American-derived genres. For him, the political thriller is little more than a borrowing of 'the dramatic recipes (plot revelations, palpitating suspense, traditional heroes) of the American-style detective story', which is then merely injected with a political theme (1974: 29). However, Hennebelle's general dismissal of the political thriller needs a little more consideration due to the fact that, as Hayward has noted, the events of May 1968 and their aftermath led to shifts within mainstream cinema, beyond simply the thriller, that in turn provided an impetus for the inclusion of a wider range of political subject matter. She argues that these included 'political scandals and affairs ... high finance and fraud' as well as 'the politics of paranoia', a paranoia that for Hayward 'Was not unjustified given the climate of the times when police powers – including the brutality of the CRS [*Compagnies Républicaines de Sécurité*] during the May 1968 demonstrations – were still very unrestricted and the state had total autocracy over the audio visual media' (2005: 239–240). The political thriller was therefore not the only manifestation of political themes in the mainstream cinema of the period, but given the points made by Hayward, it seems a particularly appropriate vehicle to consider some of these concerns.

Other influences on the development of the political thriller in France

Beyond the events of May '68, it is also important to acknowledge some of the wider influences on the development of the political thriller in France. For example, as will be touched on later in this dossier, there were political filmmaking trends within other national cinemas, such as the work of Francesco Rosi and Gillo Pontecorvo in Italy, that it can be argued were highly influential on the concept of the political thriller.

In addition, other traditions within French cinema also impacted upon the adoption of the form of the thriller by politically motivated filmmakers at the end of the 1960s and into the 1970s. For example, as Susan Hayward notes, many of the main trends within French filmmaking of the 1930s advocated a 'popular, even populist cinema' (2005: 144). One of the major trends that she identifies in this regard is the 'realist cinema' of the era that encompassed both social realism and poetic realism. Amongst these works were films that centred on crime stories and were infused with the leftist politics of the day, in particular, those of the Popular Front, a coalition of the left that encompassed communists, socialists and radicals and who were victorious in the legislative elections in 1936. These trends, therefore, also offered models of politicised filmmakers, such as Jean Renoir and Marcel Carné, choosing to use accessible cinematic forms.

After World War II, a number of filmmakers would continue to attempt to address a range of social and political issues facing France within their work. A good example of this tendency is André Cayatte, whose work can certainly be seen as a precursor to the political thrillers of the 1970s. Hayward describes his work as focusing on 'social and judiciary issues' and being 'very popular with audiences' (2005: 186). In the 1950s, Cayatte's work explored a series of social issues in a commercially appealing form. These included: euthanasia and the ability to judge those involved in *La Justice est faite* (*Justice Is Done*, 1950); the complex issues surrounding the death penalty in *Nous sommes tous des assassins* (*Are We All Murderers*, 1951); juvenile delinquency and its social and political causes in *Avant le déluge* (*Before the Deluge*, 1954);

and the problems in the process of the justice system in *Le Dossier noir* (*Black Dossier*, 1955) (Hayward, 2005: 186–187).

Writing in *Cahiers du Cinema* in June 1954, André Bazin saw the significance in Cayatte's work. He stated:

> The Auteur of *Before the Deluge* (1955) introduced into French cinema a new kind of social film, which has imposed itself with such force that it has inspired numerous mutations in more or less attenuated or exaggerated form. There is no denying that *Justice is Done* (1950) and *We are all Murderers* (1952) have changed the course of French film production.
>
> 2002: 3

Perhaps not surprisingly given this pedigree, in the 1970s Cayatte would also contribute to the cycle of political thrillers of the decade with *Il n'y a pas de fumée sans feu* (*There's No Smoke without Fire*, 1973), which focuses on the fallout from the publication of photographs of a political candidate's wife attending a sex party, and *La raison d'état* (*State Reasons*, 1978), which explores the arms trade.

Political émigrés

Another group of politically motivated Hollywood filmmakers arrived in France during the 1950s. It was made up of émigrés from the anti-communist activities of the House Un-American Activities Committee (HUAC) in the USA who were seeking work following their blacklisting due to their left-wing sympathies. Together, they formed a small colony of American practitioners, including Jules Dassin, Ben and Norma Barzman, Betsy Blair and John Berry, who found support and sympathy from those involved in the French film industry such as high-profile actors Simone Signoret and Yves Montand. Due to their experiences in Hollywood, members of this group brought an American sensibility in terms of style and story to French cinema, and their work can be seen as an influence on those in France, and elsewhere, who wanted to make political work that had mainstream appeal.

As Rebecca Prime argues, filmmakers such as Jules Dassin represented a link between the style of American cinema and that of the poetic realism so dominant in French left-wing filmmaking in the 1930s. She states, discussing his French-made heist film *Rififi* (1955):

> Rather than use his Hollywood know-how to make superlative spoofs of American films, Dassin expressed his admiration for Italian neorealism and documentary aesthetics through his lyrical depiction of Paris's grandeur and grit. Along with Jacques Becker's *Touchez pas au grisbi* (1954) and Jean-Pierre Melville's *Bob le Flambeur* (1956), *Rififi* represents a continuation of the pre-war tradition established in films such as *La Nuit du Carrefour* (dir. Jean Renoir, 1932), *Pépé le Moko* (dir. Julien Duvivier, 1937) and *Le Dernier Tournant* (dir. Pierre Chenal, 1939).
>
> 2014: 179

The influence of the films and filmmakers that combined the mainstream narrative strategies of Hollywood cinema with left-wing ideas can certainly be felt in terms of the form of the political thriller in France and across Europe. Émigré practitioners would use their experience of mainstream filmmaking to become involved in the production of political thrillers in France. For example, as shall be discussed in a later chapter, Ben Barzman worked without credit on *Z* and was one of the screenwriters of *L' Attentat* (*Plot*, Boisset, 1972).

Another interesting example of a film directed by a Hollywood émigré that in some manner uses the form of the political thriller is *Monsieur Klein* (1976). The film was made by Joseph Losey, who by the 1970s had become one of the highest-profile political émigrés to Europe because of the Hollywood blacklist. He had spent much of the late 1950s and 1960s working out of the UK, initially under pseudonyms such as Victor Hanbury and Alec C. Snowden before finding critical success under his own name with a series of high-profile collaborations with the writer Harold Pinter that included *The Servant* (1963), *Accident* (1967) and *The Go-Between* (1971). These films had brought Losey a critical reputation as a filmmaker who could make thoughtful films that also appealed to audiences. In the 1970s, this brought him the opportunity to work in France.

Starring Alain Delon, one of the most bankable stars of the 1970s in France, *Monsieur Klein* explores the life of a seemingly apolitical man who gets embroiled in the events leading up to the Paris round-up of Jews in 1942, possibly due to a case of mistaken identity. The film avoids any clear-cut explanation of the mix-up and its subsequent impact upon Klein's life, perhaps preventing some of the pleasures of the thriller form. In this regard, it is interesting to note, as Rachel Hayward does in the chapter on *Special Section* (*Section spéciale*, 1975), that the project had originally been assigned to Costa-Gavras to direct and that one of the writers was Italian Franco Solinas, who collaborated with this director on the political thriller *State of Siege* (*État de siège*, 1972) earlier in the decade. Both filmmakers will be discussed more in the following chapter, but their involvement in the development of *Monsieur Klein* perhaps explains the use of 'thriller' elements of the film, particularly the plot device of potentially mistaken identity. Indeed, it is possible to imagine, if it had in fact been completed by Costa-Gavras, a version of the film that foregrounds much more such suspense devices in the plot. Losey would continue to work with French-based left-wing practitioners when he directed *Roads to the South* (*Les Routes du Sud*, 1978), which was written in an autobiographical fashion by Jorge Semprún and starred Yves Montand, both of whom by this point had become very significant figures on the French and European cultural left.

The presence of blacklisted Hollywood filmmakers in France (and Europe more generally) also had a significant impact on some of those French filmmakers who, during the 1970s, were looking at ways to make their own political films. One such practitioner was Bertrand Tavernier, whose debut film *The Watchmaker of St. Paul* (*L'Horloger de Saint-Paul*, 1974) might be considered as something of a politicised thriller. When interviewed by *Cineaste* magazine in 1978, Tavernier discussed his politics. He said that he still saw himself as a Trotskyist and that he was still very much interested in politics (on other occasions, the director talked of being close to the Trotskyist Internationalist Communist Organisation). In this interview, he articulates the influence of the Hollywood films made by those who would be blacklisted in the post-war witch-hunts. In one of his previous roles within the film industry, as a press agent, he remembers:

> I did a lot of work on the Blacklist. I met people who influenced me, like Abraham Polonsky, Dalton Trumbo and Herbert Bierman ... I

was fascinated by what you call the 'liberal movement' in Hollywood – Joseph Losey, John Berry and Carl Foreman – and how that movement was destroyed.

1983: 228

As well as his own films, Tavernier would also produce the work of other politically committed filmmakers in the 1970s, for example, *La question* (*The Question*, 1977), directed by his former assistant Laurent Heynemann, a film that explores the use of torture by the French army in Algeria. In the *Cineaste* interview, Tavernier uses the fact that he is supporting the efforts of a Communist filmmaker, that is, one close to the Communist Party, to call for a broader, more sympathetic, leftist-critical approach to political filmmaking. In particular, it seems that he is arguing for a more positive response to the more formally commercial political films produced in France that had been dismissed by some on the left, such as Guy Hennebelle. He put it thus:

> The worst thing now is all the barriers between the left factions and movements; you have the Maoists who want to destroy the Trotskyists and they in turn want to destroy the communists. I'm tired of leftists dismissing, with words like 'horrible', the films of other leftists. One should keep some of the adjectives like 'disgusting' for the real reactionary films. I'm interested in all kinds of political films – commercial and militant – and I feel the militant film director can learn from me, just as I can learn from his work.
>
> 1983: 231

This argument is a direct questioning of the critical dismissal of politically motivated leftist films, such as the political thrillers discussed in this book, due to political dogma.

Political violence

As with other political thrillers produced across Europe, particularly in West Germany and Italy, another key concern of films produced in France during the 1970s was the growing tendency towards violence and terrorism that was becoming commonplace on both sides of the political divide. For a number of filmmakers, this meant creating work that offered a critical reflection on left-wing political violence and terrorist actions.

The development of the political thriller

One director and screenwriter who attempted to address the issues associated with this was Claude Chabrol. Chabrol had a long association with the thriller form and had been widely referred to as creating films in the mould of Alfred Hitchcock (see Hayward, 2005: 258, for example). His work in the late 1960s and early 1970s, most notably *Les Biches* (1968) and *Le Boucher (The Butcher,* 1970), had consistently criticised the morality of the French bourgeoise. As the 1970s progressed, his films became more explicitly political, firstly with *Les Noces rouges (Wedding in Blood)* in 1973 and then even more explicitly in 1974 with *Nada*. The latter film was an adaptation of the novel of the same name by Jean-Patrick Manchette, a renowned leftist crime writer whose works often used the form of the thriller or crime story to criticise the social order in France and the operations of the state. Reviewing it at the time of its UK release, *Time Out* described Chabrol's adaptation as 'a chillingly cool political thriller'.

Nada also reflected the co-production culture of the time and the manner in which political films would be constructed to create appeal beyond France. In this instance, one could argue that by this point in the 1970s, the political thriller was now seen by producers as an example of a 'bankable' trend across Europe. The casting of Italian actor Fabio Testi as Diaz, a member of the gang of terrorists, also reflects the potential marketability of this political film outside France. Following his appearance in *The Garden of the Finzi-Continis* (Vittorio De Sica, 1970), Testi was becoming a popular actor in Italy, playing the lead in a number of Italian genre pieces including the crime films *Gang War in Naples (Camorra,* Pasquale Squitieri, 1972) and *Blood in the Streets* (Sergio Sollima, 1973). His inclusion in *Nada* certainly would make the film more appealing to Italian audiences.

Nada focuses on the activities of a left-wing terrorist group, the Nada of the title, following their planning and kidnapping of the American ambassador to France and the subsequent shoot-out with the police following a siege at their remote hide-out. Throughout the film, one of the noteworthy aspects is the discussions of strategy within the Nada group, which is made up of anarchists and other affiliated left-wing activists. This reflects the wider discussions taking place in society around the use of the type of political violence that the film represents. With the events shown in *Nada*, these lead to an additional reflection on the ways in which left-wing terrorist violence can be assimilated into state narratives in order to alienate wider elements of the population from the left's cause. As Guy Austin argues:

> By the end of the film, the French state has turned the murder of the American ambassador and the very existence of the Nada group to its own political advantage. Indeed, as the Assistant Minister explains, allowing the terrorists to kill the ambassador both alienates potential left-wing support for Nada and allows the government to replace the American with a more amenable candidate.
>
> 1999: 90

As the police move in to eliminate the group, Diaz, one of the key members of Nada, manages to escape. He records a message for those who will follow. Whilst still believing in their cause, he now rejects the group's violent actions, going on to suggest that Nada's tactics actually allowed the authorities a rationale to justify the repressive state responses to the wider population. The debates about the strategies that could be adopted by the left in their attempts to influence society that are encapsulated in a film like *Nada* certainly can also be seen to reflect the debates that circulated around the idea of the political thriller and its political effectiveness within cultural circles.

The political thriller in France that developed after the events of May '68 and drew on wider traditions of political filmmaking within French cinema would continue to offer a commercial engagement with political ideas as the 1970s progressed. However, as we have moved away from that decade, these films have become less remembered than some of the other trends of politicised filmmaking such as those represented by Jean-Luc Godard. This dossier, as was the film season it developed out of, is an attempt to bring these works once again to audiences and to position them as significant contributions to a politicised European film culture of the 1970s. The role of French cinema in this is reflected by the sheer breadth and depth of political thrillers produced by the country's film industry across the 1970s.

References

Austin, G. (1999). *Claude Chabrol*. Manchester: Manchester University Press.
Bazin, A. (2002). 'Three Forgotten French Filmmakers: André Cayatte, Georges Rouquier, and Roger Leenhardt' (B. Cardullo, Trans.). *Cinema Journal*, 42(1), 3–20.
Hayward, S. (2005). *French National Cinema* (2nd ed.). London: Routledge.
Hennebelle, G. (1974). 'Z Movies or What Hath Costa-Gavras Wrought?'. *Cineaste*, 6(2), 28–31.
Milne, T. (2003). 'Nada'. In J. Pym (Ed.), *Time Out Film Guide*. London: Penguin, 829.
Prime, R. (2014). *Hollywood Exiles in Europe: The Blacklist and Cold War Film Culture*. New Brunswick: Rutgers University Press.
Tavernier, B. (1983). 'Blending the Personal with the Political'. In D. Georgakas and L. Rubenstein (Eds), *The Cineaste Interviews on the Art and Politics of Cinema*. Chicago: Lake View Press, 225–231.

3

Costa-Gavras, Jorge Semprún and Yves Montand: Creating a model for a 'commercial' political cinema

Andy Willis

Figure 4 *State of Siege* (1973), courtesy of KG Productions

It is widely acknowledged that one of the most significant films to emerge at the end of the 1960s, which captured audiences' attentions and could certainly be labelled a political thriller, was *Z*, directed by Costa-Gavras and written by Jorge Semprún. Together, as well as apart, the pair would have an enormous impact on the development of the form of the European political thriller as the 1970s progressed. Key to their collaboration in this period was the work they undertook on three landmark films: *Z* (1969),

The Confession (*L'aveu*, 1970) and *State of Siege* (1972), some of the most powerful political dramas of the period. As Mike Wayne has noted, this work would instigate various discussions as to the place and nature of political films that adopted commercial formats. He argues that this work:

> Generated a debate concerning the political role of film in a context of social unrest. Gavras is often credited with mapping out one option: the political thriller. This involved taking the established conventions of such entertainment forms as the thriller, the film noir, the detective genre and injecting into these films a new type of story content designed to raise political questions.
>
> 2001: 68–69

John Hill had already made similar points, noting that the form adopted by the filmmakers was intended to make their work, and by extension its political content, more accessible to a wider audience. He argued that 'The films of Costa-Gavras, beginning with his exposé of political assassinations, *Z* (1969), exemplified a model of political film-making which sought to bend mainstream Hollywood conventions to radical political ends' and 'which attempted to "sugar the pill" of radical politics with the "entertainment" provided by the conventions of the thriller' (1991: 38). In doing so, a model of the European political thriller began to develop in clear contrast to other forms of more abstract political cinema that were developing during this period of social unrest across the continent.

Costa-Gavras, the son of a Greek political activist, left his home country for Paris when he found his opportunities to attend university were limited due to his father's left-wing affiliations. *Z* was the director's third feature film following work as an assistant to high-profile filmmakers such as René Clair, Henri Verneuil and Jean Becker. He had made his directorial debut in 1965 with *The Sleeping Car Murders* (*Compartiment tueurs*), a well-received adaptation of Sébastien Japrisot's train-bound murder mystery which had been published in 1962. It was during the film's production that Costa-Gavras solidified his friendship with cast members Simone Signoret and Yves Montand. Significantly, both actors were at the time doyens of the French left and enjoyed a social circle that included many of France's leading left-wing creative talents as well as a number of exiles who had arrived in Europe as victims of the USA's anti-communist House Un-American Activities Committee (HUAC).

Now with the ability to draw on the creative talent and influences present in this social circle, Costa-Gavras began to work on features that more clearly reflected his humanitarian, anti-authoritarian and left-leaning political perspectives. As his career as a director developed, his films would also reflect a deep-rooted desire to maintain an engagement with audiences as well as contain political ideas. It was this commitment that led to him working in what can broadly be described as commercial forms. Firstly, as noted, a murder mystery with *The Sleeping Car Murders*, then, for his second feature, a war film, with the partisan drama *Shock Troops* (*1 homme de trop*, 1967). *Shock Troops* also reflected his inclination to use popular actors, in this case, Charles Vanel and Jean-Claude Brialy, who would appeal to cinema-goers. Indeed, that commitment to reaching audiences by casting popular performers who may have helped his films do so would continue when the director turned his attention to the political thriller with *Z* in 1969, a film that would mark his first collaboration with the political activist and screenwriter Jorge Semprún.

Semprún, who from 1936 was an exile with his family from the civil war in Spain, had joined the French Resistance to the Nazis in World War II in 1940 aged nineteen. As a Spaniard, he had hoped to contribute to their defeat and, as a result, weaken Franco's dictatorship in his home country. During this period, he worked for the Resistance group *Main d'oeuvre immigré* (MOI) under the alias Gérard Sorel. One of his roles with the group was collecting arms that had been dropped by the Allies in support of the Resistance's struggle (Fox Maura, 2017: 43). In 1943, Semprún was captured by the Gestapo and ultimately sent to the Buchenwald concentration camp, from which he emerged in April 1945 (Fox Maura, 2017: 95). During his time in the camp, Semprún had become close to the Communist underground, and following the war, utilising his newly acquired skills in deception and resilience, he began to operate clandestinely as an agent for the Spanish Communist Party, crossing the border between France and Spain.

By the 1960s, Semprún had also become a writer of some note. He drew on his own experiences as a prisoner during the war for

The Long Voyage, which was first published in 1963. Later in the decade, he would begin to work on screenplays for the cinema. His first major effort of note was the script for *The War Is Over* (*La guerre est finie*, 1966), directed by Alain Resnais. The film was once again based on Semprún's own experiences, drawing on his underground work for the Spanish Communist Party across the French–Spanish border. Significantly, Yves Montand, who had appeared in Costa-Gavras's *The Sleeping Car Murders*, was cast as Diego, the film's lead. The actor would become one of the writer and director's closest friends and collaborators, and as the 1960s came to an end, the first significant fruits of the creative collaboration between Semprún, Costa-Gavras and Montand, the feature film *Z*, would be released into cinemas.

Inspired by events in Greece, notably the assassination of politician Grigorios Lambrakis in 1963, and based on the 1966 novel of the same name by Greek writer Vassilis Vassilikos that covers the events around the killing, *Z* was in development before the events of May 1968 took place. However, the release of the film in Europe in early 1969 was able to benefit from audiences' increasing desire for films that dealt with political themes in the aftermath of the May events. Costa-Gavras himself was well aware of the impact of May '68 on spectators' open-mindedness when it came to films that presented politically engaged themes. Following the release of the film, he stated:

> There has been an uprising in France in 1968 and there has been a growing feeling about the war in Vietnam. The general public has become more political. The world has become much more open-minded. I think cinema has to follow this trend. More and more of our films will be political. I will make more political films.
>
> 1983: 9

The political and campaigning nature of *Z* is reflected from the very opening of the film, which begins with the statement 'Any similarity to actual events or persons living or dead is not coincidental. It is intentional' on screen. The film's plot then focuses on the investigation that follows the death of a charismatic politician, the Z of the title played by Yves Montand, who is leading the opposition to an increasingly dictatorial and militarised government. Whilst the film was based on scrupulous research, as John J. Michalczyk noted, 'The form that the scenario and film took was that of political fiction as opposed to political documentary. The account of the assassination would be well documented but also dramatized to attract a larger viewing public' (1984: 81). Costa-Gavras stated he felt that 'showing the story through the investigating judge would be the most effective way of revealing the political situation' (1983: 5). It would also prove to be a useful vehicle when it came to attracting a broad audience as it is through the use of the idea of the investigation, and the creation of a sense of an ever more consuming conspiracy, that the film is able to utilise some of the codes and conventions of the thriller.

Costa-Gavras also noted that 'we decided from the beginning that it would be a completely directed film with well-known actors playing the major roles' (1983: 5). As we shall see with a number of the films discussed in this dossier, the importance of well-known performers who had some level of box office appeal would become a key component of many of the commercial political films of the era. Therefore, across the political thriller in Europe during the 1970s, one can find a range of popular performers who appear in a number of films, including Yves Montand, Jean-Louis Trintignant, Jean Seberg, Alain Delon, Lino Ventura, Michel Piccoli, Simone Signoret and Gian Maria Volonté, all of whom bring their film stardom and box office appeal to help attract audiences to these works and hopefully engender some kind of discussion of the issues they explore on screen. Again, as Costa-Gavras argued, 'The most important thing is that it have a large audience because of the political possibilities' (1983: 8). Occasionally, the impact of the films may have manifested itself in smaller, more personal responses. Costa-Gavras recalls that following screenings of Z, 'In Paris, people left notes at the door saying that they had been to Greece and loved the land and its people very much but they would not return until the present regime fell. They transformed their outrage into a political act against the junta' (1983: 8).

Whilst Z is constructed in a manner that carefully avoids saying exactly where it is set, it is certainly possible, through reading the careful placement of objects and images in the *mise en scène* such as pictures of the Greek royal family and politicians on the walls, Greek branded beer and the aircraft that are clearly displaying the livery of Greek airlines, to conclude that the country represented is a thinly disguised version of Greece. However, the avoidance of an explicit setting also permits a political reading of Z that is both specifically about one situation, Greece, whilst also speaking to more general concerns about potential and real challenges to democracy that were taking place across the globe. Due to this, the film has the potential to be able to find a wider resonance with audiences. This in turn is greatly helped by Z's taut thriller-style plot, which slowly reveals how layers of corruption and lies prevent the truth coming to the surface and ultimately work to question whether in such situations citizens can ever trust those in positions of power, something eminently applicable to countries beyond Greece at the start of the 1970s.

As explored in the previous chapter, the form of the political thriller has been critiqued from a number of perspectives. However, from the outset, Z found some vocal supporters in the critical response to the film. Roger Ebert, reviewing the film in the *Chicago Sun-Times*, was particularly positive, describing it as 'a film of our time'. Ebert picked up on the way in which the film's story and politics could transcend the immediate setting, arguing that, for him, it had a resonance beyond being simply a story of the assassination of a Greek politician and the subsequent investigation into the events surrounding it. He stated that 'For Americans, it is about the My Lai massacre, the killing of Fred Hampton, the Bay of Pigs. It is no more about Greece than *The Battle of Algiers* was about Algeria' (Ebert, 1969). Ebert also identified the filmmaker's ability to use the form of the thriller in order to engage audiences with the events of the story. He noted that 'director Costa-Gavras has told them in a style that is almost unbearably exciting. Z is at the same time a political cry of rage and a brilliant suspense thriller. It even ends in a chase: Not through the streets but through a maze of facts, alibis and official corruption' (Ebert, 1969). For Ebert, the thriller format and the politics of the piece, and indeed the times, came together in a manner that had real impact.

For some writers, the power and impact of Z has not diminished since its original appearance on cinema screens. Looking back fifty years after its initial release, Peter Cowie stated that the film 'owes much to a certain Hollywood tradition ... of gritty, fast-moving thrillers', before going on to echo the intentions of the director and his key collaborators, when he argues that 'Costa-Gavras chose this exhilarating form deliberately, to reach as wide a public as possible and to communicate the outrage that he as a Greek felt about what was happening to his beloved country under the military junta then in power' (2019). On reflection, the choice of the style of the political thriller, the pliability of that format and its potential to initiate the discussion of ideas within audiences has meant that with *Z*, Costa-Gavras and Semprún can be seen as the creators of a model of the commercially minded political thriller, one that they and others would take, mould and use to explore a range of political ideas and situations throughout the 1970s and beyond.

The most immediate example of this continued political use of the thriller format was *The Confession* (*L'aveu*, 1970) released in France just over a year after *Z*. Another collaboration between Costa-Gavras, Semprún and Montand, *The Confession* is an adaptation of Artur London's account of how he, a former resistance fighter who became a Czech communist official, fell foul of the Soviet-backed regime and was eventually sentenced to life in prison. As the film's title suggests, it focuses on the extraction of a confession from London and follows the state-approved torture that led to it. For the central role, Costa-Gavras again turned to Montand, who fully committed to the role, losing weight and remaining distanced from his co-workers throughout the shoot. Costa-Gavras heightens the intensity of the audience's experience by creating an almost claustrophobic feeling through tight framing of Montand's emaciated and brutalised body. The resulting film is a striking condemnation of totalitarianism.

The opening of *The Confession* carefully informs the audience through dialogue and the use of images associated with both the Resistance in France and the Spanish Civil War, such as propaganda posters and Robert Capa's famous photograph of the falling soldier, that even veterans of these conflicts, and the heroes of the left, are not safe in Czechoslovakia. Montand's London states that such veterans are being rounded up and 're-educated' by the party. This early sequence suggests that audiences see London's not as an individual story but a typical and emblematic one which highlights what happened to him but, crucially, to others as well. This sequence importantly establishes what follows as the tale of a regime gone wrong, not of one man's individualist struggle against the state.

However, perhaps missing this point, the film brought criticism from some on the left who, perhaps naively, felt it was an anti-communist work that particularly betrayed Montand's former allegiances with the Communist Party in France. According to *Cineaste* magazine, *The Confession* 'stirred considerable debate in radical circles about how far one could go in denouncing Stalinism without becoming anti-communist' (Georgakas and Rubenstein, 1983: 64). Indeed, it was this debate in particular that brought Montand into conflict with the French Communist Party, which he had long had close connections to, as had other members of his family. The debate over the politics of *The Confession* brought into focus some of the questions that had been vexing Montand, Costa-Gavras and Semprún following the Soviet intervention in the Prague Spring in August 1968. That action had consolidated the already-existing concerns and growing mistrust of the Communist Party the trio had, in particular, the influence of the Soviet Communist Party internationally. Montand, specifically, had begun questioning his faith in the Communist Party following the Soviet intervention in Hungary in 1956, but his commitment to the ideals of peace and socialism had prevented him from cancelling a concert tour of Eastern Bloc cities (Moores, 1991: 139). The response to *The Confession* upon its release in France would see all three further marginalised from the Communist Party in France. The most forceful criticism of the film came from the then Communist Party newspaper *L'Humanité*, which accused the filmmakers of making an anti-communist film from a communist book. This position was undermined somewhat when the book's author Artur London declared in an interview with *Le Monde* that the film had been faithful to the spirit of the book (Montand, 1992: 370). In fact, the issues raised by the film intersected with those that had concerned the new left that was developing in the late 1960s and sought a fresh left-wing politics of compassion that did not cower from offering criticism of the Stalinist tendencies of the French, and other European, Communist Parties.

Montand's next collaboration with Costa-Gavras was another political thriller, *State of Siege*. In this instance, attention turned to the United States' interventions in Latin America, using Uruguay as a model. In this film, Montand played a CIA operative covertly 'advising' the pro-American government with regard to torture, who is subsequently kidnapped by a guerrilla group modelled on the Tupamaros. As the revolutionaries question him about his role in the country, the government unleashes death squads to counter their growing influence. Following *State of Siege*, and without Montand in a major role, Costa-Gavras and Semprún turned their attention to collaboration during the German occupation of France during World War II in *Special Section*. Once again, utilising a tension-building narrative, the film focuses on the section of the title, a group set up to select six people to be killed in response to the Resistance killing of a German officer. Both films are the subjects of chapters that follow in this dossier. Later, Costa-Gavras continued his work within the world of the political thriller, this time in America with the award-winning *Missing* (1982), *Betrayed* (1988) and *The Music Box* (1989).

References

Costa-Gavras, C. (1983). 'More and More of Our Films Will Be Political'. In D. Georgakas and L. Rubenstein (Eds), *The Cineaste Interviews: On Art and Politics of the Cinema*. Chicago: Lake View Press.
Cowie, P. (2019). 'A Film Tailor-Made for Its Times; Costa-Gavras's 'Z' Is Docudrama as Political Protest'. *Wall Street Journal*. Retrieved from: www.wsj.com/articles/a-film-tailor-made-for-its-times-11575656052
Ebert, R. (1969, 30 December). 'Z'. *Chicago Sun-Times*. Retrieved from: www.rogerebert.com/reviews/z-1969
Fox Maura, S. (2017). *Jorge Semprún: The Spaniard Who Survived the Nazis and Conquered Paris*. Brighton: Sussex Academic Press.
Georgakas, D. and Rubenstein, L. (Eds) (1983). *The Cineaste Interviews: On Art and Politics of the Cinema*. Chicago: Lake View Press.
Hill, J. (1991). 'Hidden Agenda: Politics and the Thriller'. *Circa*, 57 (May–June), 36–41.
Michalczyk, J. J. (1984). *Costa-Gavras: The Political Fiction Film*. London: Associated University Presses.
Montand, Y., Hamon, H. and Rotman, P. (1992). *You See, I Haven't Forgotten*. London: Chato and Windus.
Moores, P. M. (1991). 'Celebrities in Politics: Simone Signoret and Yves Montand'. In J. Gaffney and E. Kolinsky (Eds), *Political Culture in France and Germany: A Contemporary Perspective*. London: Routledge, 130–154.
Wayne, M. (2001). *Political Film: The Dialectics of Third Cinema*. London: Pluto Press.

4

State of Siege (*État de siège*), Costa-Gavras, 1973

Andy Willis

Figure 5 *State of Siege* (1973), courtesy of KG Productions

As with both *Z* and *The Confession*, the Costa-Gavras-directed *State of Siege* was based on real events, in this instance, the kidnapping of an American advisor, Dan A. Mitrione, by the leftist Tupamaros group in Uruguay on 31 July 1970. Mitrione was taken at the same moment as two other foreign nationals, a Brazilian and another American, and the Tupamaros called for the release of political prisoners in return for their captives' release. Later, the group announced that due to the fact that their demands had not yet been met, Mitrione had been killed. The other two captives were released. These events were the source for one of the most significant political thrillers of the 1970s.

In an interview with Peter Cowie in 2015, Costa-Gavras stated that he had first become interested in the American involvement in the affairs of other countries in the context of post-war Greece. The filmmaker noted that, during the civil war period and immediately afterwards, the American ambassador John Peurifoy had become a very influential figure, before being sent to Guatemala in 1956 where he was involved in activities aimed at destabilising the left-wing government. Peurifoy's stationing in these countries suggested a certain pattern of American intervention that could be found in many other states across the world. The story of Mitrione, why he was in Uruguay, what his role there was and why he was selected as a target for kidnapping, offered an opportunity to make a film that explored America's international activities, in this instance, their influence in Latin America. By using the example of Uruguay, in *State of Siege*, Costa-Gavras could explicitly explore issues of American neocolonialism. In an interview with *Cineaste* magazine, he stated that his aim in making the film was 'Simply to present a situation, a specific example of neocolonialism, and in so doing to show the faces of events that are hidden to the public' (1983: 65).

The Mitrione incident also raised important questions about the legitimacy of political violence. It was these issues that became increasingly central as Costa-Gavras developed the project that would eventually become *State of Siege*. One of the main things that most interested Costa-Gavras about the Mitrione incident was the fact that it raised the issue of what was at stake morally when a group such as the Tupamaros turned to politically motivated violence. At a historical moment, the early 1970s, when left-wing political violence was increasing across the world, the director and his screenwriter Franco Solinas felt the question was of growing urgency internationally. Significantly, the violence that is explored in the film is not just that involved in the killing of Mitrione, here renamed Santore and played by Yves Montand, but also in the acts which the state utilises to maintain its control, represented here in actions such as the torture of members of the political opposition, and with which it retaliates to the kidnapping by killing members of the guerrilla group.

Following detailed research that involved Costa-Gavras and Solinas meeting with a number of the Tupamaros, *State of Siege* was shot in Chile with support from the government of Salvador Allende. Following the success of Z, the director and his producers had managed to secure a budget that allowed for a film with reasonably high production values. This fact would permit the filmmakers to once again aim to make a film that had the potential to appeal to a broad audience. This was important as, for Costa-Gavras, '*State of Siege* was intended to help people gain consciousness of this reality, of this problem' (1983: 65). To achieve this, the director felt that dramatising real events, scrupulously researched, was the best approach as this appealed to cinema-goers. As he put it, 'the problem is the audience, the audience goes to see this kind of film, a dramatization' (1983: 69). Responding to the point made by the director, the interviewer from *Cineaste* magazine put it thus: 'In other words, they might not have an interest in a specific historical or political subject but would go to see the film because of the way in which it was mounted' (1983: 69). Once again in relation to Costa-Gavras's films, this brings the question of film form to the fore. The director's response, perhaps not surprising given his stated desire to reach audiences with his films, was pretty straightforward when he stated:

> In terms of this problem of form and content, I prefer to give more emphasis to the theme than to the form ... had I tried at the same time, as director, to create a second, formal difficulty for the audience, to try to show things in a new way, I would have run the risk of losing them ... so there is a choice you must make.
> 1983: 71

Key to *State of Siege*'s potential to reach a wider audience was the casting of Yves Montand. As already noted, the director and actor had worked together on numerous projects and it could be argued they were political 'fellow travellers'. For the filmmakers, he was a vital component of the strategy they adopted in terms of audience appeal, with Costa-Gavras putting it succinctly when he stated that 'you don't catch flies with vinegar. People are going to see Montand and they see something they would never have seen otherwise' (1983: 72). However, beyond that, it was Montand's very particular likability as a star that was also important to the filmmaker's stratagems. In this instance, it was the actor's appeal to audiences that the director wanted to exploit. For Costa-Gavras, with *State of Siege*:

> It was very important to have Yves Montand specifically because he's a very sympathetic person – at the beginning of the film the audience is for Yves Montand, they are not against him, they are for him. And it was extremely important for that character to be sympathetic from the beginning so that the audience could not subsequently refuse what's told in the film.
>
> 1983: 72

In the creation of the character of Santore, the filmmakers fashioned someone who was shown as a dedicated family man, someone who seemed to represent rather mainstream values. This allowed for the questions of who he actually was and what he was in the country for to be viable ones that would engage audiences. Central to ensuring these questions do not fade from the audience's consciousness is the character of the reporter Carlos Ducas, played by O. E. Hasse. His role as a journalist is pivotal to the film as it is he who is continually seen asking questions of the authorities, and in so doing becoming something of a moral guide for the audience. Even if the answers he receives are not fully forthcoming, which may be a touch too direct and simplistic for the film, the questions he posits are always in the air and so in the audience's mind. Crucial to this is his pointedly asking 'who is this ... Mr Santore, really?'

Costa-Gavras also showed an awareness that *State of Siege* might also appeal to different audiences, perhaps with different agendas, not one amorphous, undistinguished set of filmgoers. Such consciousness is significant as it suggests a great deal of self-awareness regarding how to construct a film that will work for different components of an audience. For example, he noted that, for him, 'It's also important for people who are more politicized to have a movie like this. They know what it's about but it's important to have a starting point' (1983: 65), but that for political films like his, 'the other people, the sort of people who are perhaps very surprised about these things ... are the most important, I think. I hope that when they see this movie they will start to ask questions themselves or of others' (1983: 65). Such an attitude reflects the fact that Costa-Gavras saw the film as causing debate and discussion rather than suggesting it might actually solve any of the problems or issues it represents. That debate could take place amongst these various audiences and potentially go in various directions. This reflects the intention that the film not be simple propaganda following a simple 'party line'. For the director, 'I don't think we can completely explain something, with all its ramifications and connections, in a film. I think a film is like a match or a detonator – you can make a big fire or explosion, or nothing at all. It's just the beginning of something, not the totality' (1983: 72).

The potential for *State of Siege* to ruffle political feathers was certainly felt in the USA. The film was due to have its US premiere at an event in Washington, DC to inaugurate the American Film Institute theatre at the Kennedy Centre. However, when its subject matter, the killing of a CIA 'advisor' operating in Latin America, came to light, pressure was applied for the invitation to be withdrawn. George Stevens Jr, then National Director of the American Film Institute, made a statement declaring that the film was an inappropriate choice for the event as it rationalised political assassination (Welsh, 1977: 28). *State of Siege* asked enough questions about America's neocolonial practices to be thought of as too controversial for such a high-profile event.

Again, in presenting this story, Costa-Gavras, whilst acknowledging that the film may lack conventional suspense, expressed a desire to make a film that utilised some of the conventions of the thriller. He saw this partly revolving around the question of who the central character really was, stating that in the coverage of the incident that had inspired the film, 'Mitrone was first presented as a diplomat, then a consul, then a policeman. It was puzzling, in a sense a suspense' (1983: 65). In a reflection on the film published alongside the release of a restored version of the film by Criterion, Mark Danner observed the manner in which the film may be seen as a critical engagement with the form of the thriller. He notes that *State of Siege*:

> Is not a whodunit but a how-was-it-done ... Costa-Gavras and his scriptwriter work by overthrowing the traditional lineaments of the thriller: we begin with the ending and work backward. 'We start the movie with the American being killed, we see his burial, we see the ceremony,' Costa-Gavras observed in 2009. 'The idea was not to play with that idea: he will be killed or he won't be killed. It was to

follow the story a different way ... Yes. He's dead. But who is he, and what is he doing?'.

Danner, 2015

Utilising the codes and conventions of a popular cinematic form to create a political film is something that *State of Siege*'s screenwriter Franco Solinas had also built a significant reputation for doing. As John J. Michalczyk put it writing in *Cineaste*, he always 'walked the tightrope between politicized fiction and fictionalized politics' (1984a: 30). Importantly for his aims with this project, Solinas had also developed a number of significant working relationships with directors who were also committed to creating work that could connect with mainstream audiences. As Julian Petley argued, 'his decision to work within a popular genre was a characteristically political act' (2000: 804). As a result of these collaborations, Solinas would also develop an ability to write scripts in a number of styles.

It can be argued that Solinas's most impactful collaboration was with Italian director Gillo Pontecorvo. This began with *Giovanna*, Pontecorvo's part of the portmanteau film *The Windrose* (*Die Windrose*, 1957). The pair worked together again on the adaptation of Solinas's novel *The Wide Blue Road* (*La grande strada azzurra*, 1957), which was co-directed by Maleno Malenotti and marked an early collaboration with Yves Montand, who played the lead role. It was the writer's and director's work together throughout the 1960s that would deliver their most impactful political films. These included *Kapò* (1960), about a young woman's experiences in, and attempt to escape from, a Nazi concentration camp; *The Battle of Algiers* (*La battaglia di Algeri*, 1966), which focused on the liberation struggle in Algeria and the French response to it; and *Burn!* (*Queimada*, 1969), a film about the anti-colonial struggle in the Portuguese Caribbean.

Early on in his screenwriting career, Solinas revealed an interest in working with a variety of different styles of film that had the potential to appeal to audiences. He contributed to the script for the historical drama *Vanina Vanini* (alternative title *The Betrayer*, 1961), directed by Roberto Rossellini, and the realist bandit drama *Salvatore Giuliano* (1962) for Francesco Rosi. Solinas explained, echoing points made by Costa-Gavras, why he was such a good collaborator for the director:

Movies have an accessory and not a decisive usefulness in the various events and elements that contribute to the transformation of society. It is naive to believe that you can start a revolution with a movie and even more naive to theorize about doing so. Political films are useful on the one hand if they contain a correct analysis of reality and on the other if they are made in such a way as to have that analysis reach the largest possible audience.

Petley, 2000: 805

Given this observation, it is perhaps not surprising that from the mid-1960s, Solinas chose to work on scripts for popular Italian westerns. During this period, he contributed work on the scripts for *The Big Gundown* (*La resa dei conti*, Sergio Sollima, 1966), *A Bullet for the General* (*Quien sabe?*, Damiano Damiani, 1966), *The Mercenary* (*Il mercenario*, Sergio Corbucci, 1968) and *Tepepa* (Giulio Petroni, 1969). Austin Fisher argues that Solinas's screenplays for these films mark a particular intervention in the cycle of politically motivated westerns. He states that 'The four Westerns attributed to the pen of Franco Solinas in particular signal a consistent advocacy of insurrection from a Third Worldist perspective through tales of agrarian political awakenings and violent rejection of the capitalist West' (2011: 41–42). In doing so, the westerns that Solinas worked on can be seen as exploring some of the same themes that are the focus of *State of Siege*, in particular, the interventions of nations from the West in the politics of the Global South, and how they can be resisted by local political organisations. As Fisher again remarks, this time in relation to *A Bullet for the General*, 'The resulting screenplay (*Quien sabe?*) above all addressed themes central to Solinas's contemporary oeuvre. The irreconcilable dichotomy between Western civilization and the underdeveloped Third World, the arrogance of the West's interventions in native affairs, the necessity of violent resistance against this intervention: all are explored' (2011: 131). As noted earlier, the question of the use of violence in political struggle is also something that is central to *State of Siege*. One of the most striking aspects of the film is the way that it demonstrates that the decision to kill Santore is not taken by a few political 'hotheads'.

In a sequence towards the end of *State of Siege*, that clearly draws on the codes and conventions of the thriller, Este, a member of the Tupamaros played by Jean-Luc Bideau, sits on a bus as it makes its journey across the city. At intervals, individuals who are clearly shown through their costumes to represent a variety of social groups and backgrounds join him and vote yes or no to the execution of Santore. As the votes build up, even though the audience most likely know the outcome, there is a sense that the result could go the other way, creating a sense of both tension and jeopardy. Vitally, the internal democracy of the group shown here offers the idea of a variety of responses to the situations we have been witness to throughout the film and the varied responses within the Tupamaros to them. The variety of representatives we see vote also clearly suggests that support for the Tupamaros' cause is drawn from all parts of Uruguayan life, not simply a small group of radicals. This reflects the fact that, as Michalczyk noted, when Costa-Gavras and Solinas met members of the group, they discovered that it 'did not consist of wild, alienated, anarchistic youth. The members came primarily from the middle and upper classes. They were from all walks of life – university professors and students, intellectuals, attorneys, soldiers, priests, police, artists, doctors, and other professionals. Costa-Gavras later remarked, "they are everywhere and nowhere"' (1984b: 151). This representation of resistance clearly counters Santore's earlier assertion regarding who the Tupamaros are and what their aims are when he says to his captors 'You are subversives, Communists. You want to destroy the foundations of society, the fundamental values of our Christian civilisation, the very existence of the free world. You are an enemy that must be fought in every possible way.'

In his review of *State of Siege* at the time of its release in the USA, Peter Biskind highlighted the issue that critics of the film, and the form of the political thriller more generally, raised, that is:

> By adopting a fictive, rather than a documentary approach to his subject, Costa-Gavras invites the suspicion that his film is only fiction. Despite the fact that his fiction literally conforms to the actual course of events ... this 'actual course of events' is fact only outside the world of fiction. Once it enters the world of fiction, it is no longer fact in any literal sense.
>
> 1973: 52

Whilst in this review Biskind finds a number of significant flaws, he also admits that the film has a political purpose which it achieves, noting that 'Nevertheless, *State of Siege* is an important film. For all its flaws, it will reach a large audience with a vital message' (1973: 54). As already noted, *State of Siege* in many ways epitomises the debate that took place around the idea of the 'political thriller'. That is, does the accessible form utilised by filmmakers, designed to be accessible to a larger, perhaps less politicised, audience, mean that the complexities of the political situations shown cannot be fully represented. The answer to that question is often an ideologically loaded one, with the answer depending on the political perspective of those providing it.

On one level, perhaps clearer almost fifty years later, *State of Siege* might be considered a success. It certainly did, as the filmmakers hoped, ask a number of urgent questions rather than provide fully formed answers about the situation of neocolonialism. Its ending, rather than suggesting any solution, shows a member of the Tupamaros observing the arrival of the new 'advisor' from the USA as Santore's body is repatriated. The acknowledgement, highlighted through this image, that the USA's involvement in the politics of other nations cannot be stopped by simply killing its representative is a significant one, and one that would gain more force as the 1970s and 1980s progressed, and that influence became more and more insidious. This is reflected, most notably, in the fact that Costa-Gavras and his team had shot *State of Siege* in Chile and the government of Allende, who had supported the production team in their endeavours, would themselves become the victims of that covert US intervention when they were overthrown by a CIA-backed coup in 1973. These events in turn would become the focus of one of Costa-Gavras's most effective political thrillers, *Missing*, made in 1982.

References

Biskind, P. (1973). '*State of Siege* review'. *Film Quarterly*, 27(1), 51–54.
Costa-Gavras, C. (1983). 'A Film Is Like a Match: You Can Make a Big Fire or Nothing at All'. In D. Georgakas and L. Rubenstein (Eds), *The Cineaste Interviews: On Art and Politics of the Cinema*. Chicago: Lake View Press, 64–76.
Cowie, P. (2015). 'Interview with Costa-Gavras'. *Criterion*. Retrieved from: www.criterion.com/current/posts/3584-costa-gavras-on-political-filmmaking

Danner, M. (2015, 27 May). '*State of Siege*: Their Torture, and Ours'. *Criterion*. Retrieved from: www.criterion.com/current/posts/3573-state-of-siege-their-torture-and-ours

Fisher, A. (2011). *Radical Frontiers in the Spaghetti Western: Politics, Violence and Popular Italian Cinema*. London: I. B. Tauris.

Michalczyk, J. J. (1984a). 'Franco Solinas: The Dialectic of Screenwriting'. *Cineaste*, 13(2), 30–33.

Michalczyk, J. J. (1984b). *Costa-Gavras: The Political Fiction Film*. London: Associated University Presses.

Petley, J. (2000). 'Solinas, Franco'. In S. Pendergast and T. Pendergast (Eds), *International Dictionary of Films and Filmmakers* (4th ed.). London: St. James Press, 804–805.

Welsh, J. M. (1977). 'Beyond Melodrama: Art, Politics, and *State of Siege*'. *Film Criticism*, 2(1), 24–31.

5

L'Attentat (*Plot*), Yves Boisset, 1972

Andy Willis

In his exploration of the idea of a European film noir, Andrew Spicer notes that, following the impact of the late 1960s and early 1970s films of Costa-Gavras, such as *Z* and *The Confession*, *L'Attentat* was the first major political thriller of the cycle that followed their success that was actually set in France (2007: 57). In particular, *L'Attentat*, directed by Yves Boisset, written by Ben Barzman and Basilio Franchina, and adapted by Jorge Semprún, utilises the format of the conspiracy thriller in order to explore the real-life disappearance of the Moroccan political leader Mehdi Ben Barka in 1965, an event that had caused great controversy in France, and internationally, at the time and by the early 1970s was still the focus of much political debate.

Presenting the events surrounding the Ben Barka incident, *L'Attentat*, broadly speaking, breaks into three sections. The first involves the plot to get rid of the troublesome, in the eyes of the authorities, political activist. Crucially, this is shown to involve representatives of various clandestine security forces including the American CIA, Moroccan government agents and the French secret service. The second section of the film focuses on the implementation of the plan to 'disappear' the film's version of Ben Barka, a politician called Sadiel, as he attends a meeting with television executives in Paris. The third, concluding section of the film follows the aftermath of Sadiel's disappearance as the various security forces seek to cover up their actions and attempt to get rid of any potential witnesses or unreliable collaborators who may not keep their involvement secret. *L'Attentat*, particularly in this final section, uses the thriller format to create a sense of jeopardy as the characters

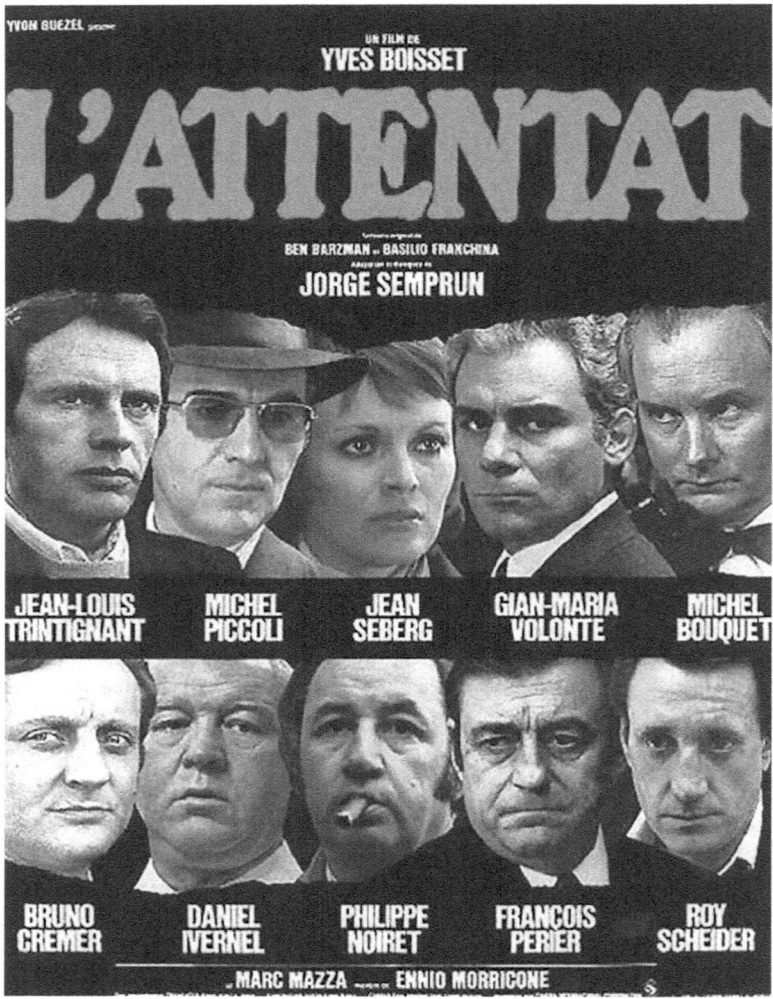

Figure 6 Advertising poster for *L'Attentat* (1972)

whom it suggests are seen as disposable in the eyes of the authorities are pursued by the agents of the killers as they seek to ensure their silence regarding the plot. The combination of politics with the codes and conventions of the thriller saw the film prove to be a box office success upon its release in France during October 1972 when, according to the AlloCiné website, it attracted a healthy 400,000 spectators.

As noted, *L'Attentat* was released in the midst of a period when audiences were seemingly receptive to political films, and in particular those that utilised commercial forms. Whilst it is widely considered that it was Costa-Gavras's *Z* (1969) that had shown the potential for such films to appeal widely to cinema-goers, it was not the only film that did so. For example, even though it had been a success at the 1966 Venice film festival, *The Battle of Algiers* (Gillo Pontecorvo, 1966) was not released commercially in France until 1970. As Patricia Caillé notes:

> The 'national' release of *The Battle of Algiers* started in the summer of 1970 in the provinces and in October 1971 in Paris where it was screened less widely than initially planned, in one, then up to four cinemas. Screenings were sporadically disrupted but the film went to the end of its run with a very steady stream of spectators.
>
> 2007: 379–380

So, alongside the high profile given to the recent work of Costa-Gavras, this factor further reveals how audiences were ready for a variety of accessible politicised films, particularly if they, as *The Battle of Algiers* did, focused on something that related directly to French politics. Alison Smith goes so far as to suggest that the cycle of political thrillers that followed in the wake of *Z* was referred to within France, perhaps somewhat negatively, as *Série-Z* (2005: 35). The use of this term suggests a clear awareness within the popular imagination of such commercial and political films being in the mould of Costa-Gavras's landmark work. However, it would be wrong to see the success of *Z* as the only indication that there was an appetite for political films amongst audiences at this historical moment, particularly in France. Indeed, it was the number of filmmakers from across Europe and beyond who continued to embrace the form of the political thriller that showed what was seen as the real potential of the form, both aesthetically and commercially.

As noted, *L'Attentat* is widely acknowledged to be broadly based on the case of Mehdi Ben Barka who 'disappeared' in Paris in 1965 and whose body was never found. Ben Barka had been a leading light of the Moroccan independence movement after World War II, and in 1959, he had helped create the National Union of Popular Forces. In 1963, he was exiled from Morocco after being accused of plotting against the King, Hassan II. From that moment, Barka moved around the globe meeting various revolutionary and left-wing leaders such as Che Guevara and Malcolm X. As one of the driving forces behind the Tricontinental Conference, which would take place in Havana in 1966, Ben Barka had become widely seen as a major figure in the international post-colonial struggle. In 1965, he left Geneva, where he was based at the time, for Paris. As *TIME* magazine put it in 1975:

> On the gray afternoon of Oct. 29, 1965, Mehdi Ben Barka – a self-exiled left-wing Moroccan politician and a well-known critic of King Hassan II – was stopped outside the Brasserie Lipp on Paris's Boulevard St. Germain by two French agents. 'You have a rendezvous with some politicians,' said one of them. Ben Barka, 45, who was accustomed to being tailed by the police, climbed into the back of an unmarked Peugeot 403. The car drove off. Ben Barka has not been seen in public since.

Ben Barka's disappearance and presumed death had been a source of great controversy within France, with President De Gaulle going so far as to deny any official French involvement in the incident. In 1972, when *L'Attentat* was released, many of the events surrounding his disappearance were still shrouded in mystery. The filmmakers behind *L'Attentat* posited a 'fictional' story that offered an explanation of these events, utilising the form of the thriller to develop a film that both questioned international governments' involvement in the planning and carrying out of the plot and through its cinematic form drew its audience into the idea of that it could have been a political conspiracy. The film utilises factual information, such as choosing to shoot the abduction scene outside the Brasserie Lipp from where Ben Barka had actually disappeared, in order to give the film and its version of events an anchor in reality. Olaf Möller, writing about Boisset's contribution to the political thriller more generally, has noted that the director felt justified in the film's interpretation of events, stating that 'In his autobiography, Boisset mentions an operative [working on behalf of the French government] gleefully telling him that *L'Attentat* had gotten everything right, although nobody involved would admit to it' (2014: 14). For this director, like Costa-Gavras, getting the events on screen in a manner that had, in their eyes, a fidelity to the real was vitally important to the credibility of their work even when it was presented in a fictional form.

At the time of its release, perhaps as a way of mitigating charges of falsification of events and the creation of imaginary characters, Boisset was keen to remind people that *L'Attentat* should also be seen as fiction, albeit fiction that he clearly wanted to ask pointed questions of the authorities and those working in their interests. At the time of the film's release, *Variety* reported that he 'claims the picture is meant to reflect on the use of assassination as a political weapon in general. He maintains it should be judged as a fiction film which hopefully would make audiences think and ask questions of themselves and their governmental reps' (1972: 30). French audiences were indeed invited to consider such issues as well as judge the 'fiction' against what was at the time in the public realm. Again, *Variety* noted this was facilitated by coverage of the film in the French press when they reported 'The leftist but non-aligned weekly, *Le Nouvel Observateur*, ran six pages on the actual historical aspects of the film. Paris dailies also gave the pic a phenomenal amount of free space' (1972: 30). Clearly then, in 1972, the disappearance of Ben Barka was still newsworthy and a film that addressed the incident was subject to a high level of scrutiny.

Variety also noted that the director was conscious that he wanted to construct a film that had the potential to appeal to a wide audience. As well as adopting the mode of the political thriller and focusing on the idea of a conspiracy, they noted 'Boisset also said that he decided to do it with top names to get better outlets and to make money' (1972: 30). This included a range of top French and international names, a number of whom had left-wing associations and had appeared in films with a leftist tone. These included Jean-Louis Trintignant, Jean Seberg, Gian Maria Volonté, Michel Piccoli, Roy Scheider, Daniel Ivernel and François Perier. Each already had a proven appeal to French audiences as well as those across Europe. Trintignant was a versatile actor and had played the lead in *Z* amongst numerous other successful works that crossed the boundaries between European art cinema, such as *The Conformist* (*Il conformista*, Bernardo Bertolucci, 1970), and popular films such as the Italian western *The Great Silence* (*Il grande silenzio*, Sergio Corbucci, 1968). Having begun her career in Hollywood, Seberg had proved popular in France following her appearance in Jean-Luc Godard's *À bout de souffle* (*Breathless*, 1960) and at the time of making *L'Attentat* was already being hounded by the FBI for her vocal support of political activist groups such as the Black Panthers. Like Trintignant, Volonté had appeared in both popular successes, such as the Italian westerns *A Fistful of Dollars* (Sergio Leone, 1964) and *For a Few Dollars More* (Sergio Leone, 1965), and more formally challenging and politicised works such as the Dziga Vertov Group's *Le Vent d'est* (1970), which drew on the actor's history of appearing in European westerns. Prior to working on *L'Attentat*, Michel Piccoli had established himself as a key actor within European cinema by collaborating with the likes of Luis Buñuel (*Belle de Jour*, 1967) and as a regular in the challenging films of Marco Ferreri (*Dillinger è morto* (*Dillinger Is Dead*), 1969). Playing a key role, as an American journalist who is revealed to be an assassin, was the American actor Roy Scheider. By the time of the release of *L'Attentat*, Scheider had already appeared in the popular *The French Connection* (William Friedkin, 1971), which had been a huge international success as well as earning him an Oscar nomination for Best Supporting Actor. Together, the cast offered a formidable range of appeal to various film audiences and would certainly, at least on paper, offer a good chance of achieving Boisset's aim of getting his political thriller into better cinemas and making some money. The appeal of such a collection of performers is reflected in the French poster for the film that clearly leads with, in the context of France, the all-star cast and gives little or no sense of what the film may be about. Further reflecting the importance of the cast to the film's marketing, its director, Boisset, and one of the screenwriters, Semprún, who had of course worked extensively with Costa-Gavras on high-profile projects and was a known presence in French cultural circles, are given a small presence beside the faces of the array of stars who stare out of the poster.

Whilst the small credit given to the film's screenwriters on the French poster reflects the fact that they were not offered to audiences as evidence of the film's high production values, they do certainly contribute to its potential appeal, bringing as they do a clear commitment to a political cinema that has the ability to connect with broad, popular audiences. One of the key writers who worked on the original drafts of *L'Attentat* was Ben Barzman, a Canadian blacklisted by Hollywood in the post-war Red Scare and who had contributed, uncredited, to the development of the script of *Z*. In 1949, he and his wife Norma, also a screenwriter, had left the USA to write on a project in London, after which he found himself unable to return to America to work because of the activities of the House Un-American Activities Committee (HUAC). The pair would initially remain in London before later relocating to France, initially basing themselves in Paris. There, the couple would find they were part of a small community of political exiles who entered into the orbit of a local artistic group associated with left-wing thinking and broadly linked to the politics of the French Communist Party. Rebecca Prime notes:

> Arriving in France at a time when the influence of the French Communist Party was at its peak, the Hollywood exiles found that their political orientation provided them with a sense of belonging to a broader community. Although no longer Party members, 'we continued to feel like Communists', Norma Barzman recalls. 'And since we were in a country where the Communist Party was a mass party, winning a large bloc of votes, we felt part of the mainstream.'
>
> 2008: 477

In Europe, one of the first projects that Ben Barzman was linked to was a production originally called *A Bottle of Milk* that had another Hollywood exile, Joseph Losey, attached to it as director. However, as Prime notes, 'Losey was unhappy with Ben Barzman's script, which in his opinion "suffered from the fact that Barzman was still a Hollywood-oriented writer"' (2008: 476–477). This observation is significant as it indicates that the writing style of Barzman was still aimed at connecting and communicating with a more mainstream audience. Losey, as already noted, on the other hand, would increasingly move more into the realm of the European art film in the 1960s. It was Barzman's experience, gained working on films that were able to connect with popular audiences, that would make him an appealing collaborator for those wanting to make political films that also had the potential to appeal to a wide range of filmgoers.

Reflecting the times, the *A Bottle of Milk* project eventually became *Stranger on the Prowl*, released in 1952 and credited as written and directed by Andrea Forzano in order to avoid the unwanted connection to the blacklisted participants who contributed to its creation. Throughout the 1950s, Barzman would continue to collaborate with Hollywood exiles on projects based in Europe. These would include an uncredited John Berry (*It Happened in Paris*, 1952), Jules Dassin (*He Who Must Die*, 1957) and, once again, Joseph Losey (*Blind Date*, 1959). Following these, Barzman would work on a number of scripts for large-scale blockbusters made in Europe by the Hollywood director Anthony Mann. These included *El Cid* (1961), *The Fall of the Roman Empire* (1964) and *The Heroes of Telemark* (1965). At first, he was unable to be credited due to the blacklist, but by the time of its release, his name was able to appear on the credits of *The Fall of the Roman Empire*.

Towards the end of the 1960s, Barzman would work, ultimately uncredited, on the development of the script for *Z*. This is perhaps not surprising given that since their arrival in Paris, the Barzmans had enjoyed the friendship of Yves Montand and Simone Signoret, who at the time were also close to a number of the Hollywood émigrés. As discussed in Chapter 2, Montand and Signoret had also been instrumental in developing the careers of both director Costa-Gavras and the credited scriptwriter of *Z* Jorge Semprún. When interviewed about Ben Barzman's work on the film, Norma Barzman recalled:

> Ben and I read the screenplay and thought it was awful. Jacques [Perrin], who was producing, and Costa[-Gavras] came to Mougins. Ben told them what he thought was wrong with it. They asked his advice. Ben came up to the bedroom to ask me what he should tell them. I said that they should just go back to the book, which was wonderful. He told them that. They threw out their screenplay. Ben did an adaptation that followed the documentary nature of the book. Jorge Semprún rewrote and took a sole credit. Nevertheless, Ben helped them make a deal with the Algerians, permitting the movie to be shot there.
>
> Ceplair, 1997: 24

If Norma Barzman's tone suggests she was unhappy with the outcome of the credits for *Z*, her husband's path would cross that of Semprún again with *L'Attentat*. Barzman worked on the development of the original script for *L'Attentat* with the Italian scriptwriter Basilio Franchina. Franchina had made his name in Italy after

World War II, where he had been responsible for the idea behind the landmark *Germany Year Zero* (Roberto Rossellini, 1948) and had gone on to be credited alongside Barzman on the scripts for *The Fall of the Roman Empire* (1964) and *The Blue Max* (1966). The final version of the script for *L'Attentat* would be credited to Semprún, which, whilst maybe frustrating for Norma Barzman, would seal the sense of this being a prestige, left-wing production of the highest credentials.

With this list of practitioners who contributed to its creation, it is not at all surprising that the politics of *L'Attentat* is clearly that of the left. The film makes a number of general points about the ability of the state, acting in the interests of international forces, to kill those who protest their actions and lead protests and opposition. It clearly engages with the post-May '68 and post-colonial moment in France. The film uses the central character of flawed leftist François Darien, played by Jean-Louis Trintignant, a friend and admirer of Sadiel but the one who ultimately sells him out, as a way to allow audiences to understand the strategies of the plotters and invite them to ask critical questions about their actions. Darien is misguidedly someone who believes he can continue to act in a way that benefits the struggle he supports, even when acting for the forces that are operating to negate its influence. Whilst he states that he still adheres to his ideals, it is made clear to the audience that he is compromised by his actions as the French secret service have a file on him and as they ask in the opening scenes, 'You can put pressure on anyone; do we have a file on him?' It is the information in the file that is used to pressure Darien into becoming part of the conspiracy. Yet, due to his engagement with the plot, he is the character who allows the audience an insight into the mindset of the conspirators. At one point, he says to one of them 'You're still seeing to it that Africa will stay French.' Whilst certainly a film that can be considered a political thriller of the left, beyond the moments when Sadiel offers an analysis of French policies in relation to its former colonies and articulates support for pan-Arab and pan-African initiatives, it is possible to argue that *L'Attentat* does not offer any real political analysis of the events surrounding Ben Barka's disappearance. The aim of the film seems to be more about inviting questions surrounding the Ben Barka affair and offering some suggestions regarding who was involved and why, rather than exploring some of the wider political potential of the story of the assassination. Whilst his work is still not as well known as maybe it should be outside France, Yves Boisset would continue to work steadily in the realm of films that dealt with real political situations as the 1970s progressed. For example, set in 1956, *R.A.S.* (1973) involves the activities of the French military in Algeria, following three soldiers, from differing political backgrounds, who become part of a disciplinary unit. *Dupont Lajoie* (*The Common Man*, 1975) shows how, after a rape and murder take place near a campsite, people are all to easily ready to make racist assumptions and blame the easy target of immigrants, whilst *Le Juge Fayard dit Le Shériff* (*Judge Fayard Called the Sheriff*, 1977) is based on another unsolved case, the 1975 killing of François Renaud, the first judge to be assassinated in France following World War II. All these films, like *L'Attentat*, represent attempts to make films that connect with audiences and explore urgent political ideas, even if on reflection they often lack the sophistication in terms of filmmaking style that is displayed by the work of Costa-Gavras.

References

AlloCiné. Retrieved from: www.allocine.fr/film/fichefilm_gen_cfilm=4340.html
Caillé, P. (2007). 'The Illegitimate Legitimacy of *The Battle of Algiers* in French Film Culture'. *Interventions: International Journal of Postcolonial Studies*, 9, 371–388.
Ceplair, L. (1997). 'Norma Barzman (and Ben Barzman)'. In P. McGilligan and P. Buhle (Eds), *Tender Comrades: A Backstory of the Hollywood Blacklist*. Minneapolis: University of Minnesota Press, 1–27.
Möller, O. (2014). 'The Path of Most Resistance: Thriller Specialist Yves Boisset Has a Knack for Pointing Out Awkward Political Truths'. *Film Comment*, 50(2), 14–15.
Prime, R. (2008). ' "The Old Bogey": The Hollywood Blacklist in Europe'. *Film History*, 20, 474–486.
Smith, A. (2005). *French Cinema in the 1970s: The Echoes of May*. Manchester: Manchester University Press.
Spicer, A. (2007). *European Film Noir*. Manchester: Manchester University Press.
TIME (1975). 'Espionage: The Murder of Mehdi Ben Barka'. 29 December.
Variety. (1972, 25 October), 30.

6

Special Section (Section spéciale), Costa-Gavras, 1975

Rachel Hayward

Figure 7 *Special Section* (1975), courtesy of The Festival Agency (Paris)

Costa-Gavras's 1975 film *Special Section* continued the director's politically engaged filmmaking and saw him once again working with writer Jorge Semprún. *Special Section* was selected for the 1975 Cannes Film Festival, where it won Costa-Gavras the award for Best Director. As was customary for the director's political thrillers, the film portrays actual events, though there is an important distinction between the preceding films, such as *Z* (1969), *The Confession* (1970) and *State of Siege* (1972), and *Special Section* in this regard: the critical spotlight is on France, Costa-Gavras's adopted homeland, whereas he had previously interrogated the regimes of other countries. This French historical focus may be a factor in the film having a less favourable reaction from audiences and critics than Costa-Gavras's previous work. *Special Section* is an adaptation of the 1973 investigatory book *L'affaire de la Section Spéciale* by Hervé Villeré, and as well as providing historical information, this essential resource informs some of the filmmakers' artistic decisions for the film.

Special Section is set in occupied France in 1941, a year after France's military defeat to Germany, and focuses on the collaborationist Vichy regime, specifically, its judicial procedures. The sequence of events depicted in the film took place over just seven days in August. Following a demonstration in Paris, two young communist protesters, Samuel Tyszelman and Henri Gautherot, are executed by a Nazi firing squad. Their comrades decide to exact revenge by targeting German soldiers, and we later learn that the Communist Party has called for twenty Germans to be killed. The first victim is naval officer cadet Alfons Moser, shot by Pierre 'Fredo' Georges and Gilbert Brustlein. In turn, the occupying forces require six deaths as retribution, and the Vichy government agrees and even offers to carry out public executions, an act not requested nor approved by the German occupying forces. As the perpetrators of the German's murder had not been caught, special courts were quickly established in order to construct a new legal framework with 'retroactive' legislation that would allow for the resentencing of already-convicted prisoners in order to fulfil the obligation to the occupying forces. The Special Section of the film's title is made up of judges chosen either for their allegiance to the authoritarian Vichy Head of State, Marshal Pétain, or, for some, their personal ambitions towards gaining a promotion. The orchestration of the courts by the Minister of the Interior, Pierre Pucheu, played by Michael Lonsdale, and the compliance of the Special Section, demonstrate not only some of the anti-Semitic and anti-communist actions of the Vichy regime but also the manipulation of the legal system in order to perform those activities.

With its focus on the legal system, *Special Section* is a rather different viewing experience than audiences had come to expect from Costa-Gavras. He makes use of some thriller conventions in the film but deviates enough from the Costa-Gavras/Semprún model of filmmaking, as outlined by Andy Willis in Chapter 3, that critics at the time of release raised questions about the film's efficacy as a political thriller and as a piece of popular cinema. The scene most aligned with thriller genre conventions is Moser's assassination at the Barbès Metro station, which takes place early in the film. This has all the heightened suspense that would be anticipated in the build-up to an on-screen killing, and the tense sequence includes identifying a victim, the shooting itself – in slow motion for heightened impact – and a chase as the perpetrators make their escape. Costa-Gavras manipulates the film's sound when Moser is shot: we hear the gunfire, but Moser's scream is silent, as are the reactions of bystanders. Diegetic sound is replaced entirely by the distorted soundtrack, which had been used to slowly build tension throughout the scene. The sound only returns to normal when Brustlein and Fredo have exited the Metro following their slow-motion chase sequence. In this example, we can see that Costa-Gavras's fidelity to the serious and detailed source material does not preclude tension on screen. Villeré's account of the assassination and especially its immediate aftermath provides evocative details, which Costa-Gavras transposes into his account of the events. Note the comparison of presenting sound and movement in this extract and Costa-Gavras's rendering of the scene:

> Still fascinated by the incident, Brustlein had not moved. He stayed still, frozen to the spot, gun in hand, when he heard someone shout: 'Stop him, stop him'. He turned and saw that Fredo had already put his gun back in his pocket and was running towards the steps leading to the station exit.
>
> Villeré, 1973: 168[1]

Costa-Gavras's route to making *Special Section* began in 1973 with his work alongside Franco Solinas on a script for *Monsieur Klein*, a project focusing on anti-Semitism in Vichy France. As Costa-Gavras describes in his autobiography, the writing duo invested a significant amount of time in developing ideas and researching the history of the period (2018: 262). As well as working with Solinas on the script, Costa-Gavras was originally due to direct and had verbally agreed with the producers that Jean-Paul Belmondo would take the lead role in *Monsieur Klein*. However, disagreements over finances and the subsequent involvement of lawyers meant that Belmondo pulled out of the project, followed by Costa-Gavras (2018: 264). Whilst Costa-Gavras did not realise that project (it was finally directed by Joseph Losey and released in 1976 starring Alan Delon), the experience of researching and developing the period had a significant impact on the director: 'I had tried to put myself in those situations, to understand the psychology and behaviour of these people. All these ghosts of the past, and the desire to write a film, still haunted me' (Costa-Gravas, 2018: 265).[2] He goes on to explain that directing *Special Section* was a suggestion from actor and producer Jacques Perrin, who was aware of the director's interest in the occupation and had recently optioned *L'affaire de la Section Spéciale*. Villeré's text is based on meticulous research and is incredibly detailed in its documentation of the people and events of the time. He strikes a balance between the personal and the official, offering an account of assassination victim Moser's last breakfast, for example (Villeré, 1973: 165). The book also includes copies of original archive documents, notably, from sources outside of France. The absence of official French documents is flagged at the beginning of the text by the inclusion of correspondence from 1972 between Villeré's publisher and the French Ministry of Justice, the latter refusing the writer's request of access to French official files for research (Villeré, 1973: 16–18). This correspondence, whilst presented factually and without comment, can easily be read as critical of the official French response to confronting the past. Once Perrin, Costa-Gavras and Semprún had decided to make the film together, they also took the decision to make it a very close adaptation of Villeré's book, and not only does the text provide the factual content for the film but also much of the dialogue. Costa-Gavras's desire for accuracy extends to the precise use of locations and the use of Vichy residents as extras.

As part of the filmmakers' usual rigorous process, they also carried out additional research for the film, including accessing interview tapes recorded clandestinely by Villeré during his investigative work (Michalczyk, 1984: 194). Addressing collaboration remained uncomfortable for many, though French society was beginning to tackle more directly the country's wartime history, with cultural representations beyond the heroic Resistance fighter appearing in cinemas. As Alison Smith writes, 'by 1975 the shock of *Le Chagrin et la pitié* (1971) [sic] was past and revelations about collaboration were already beginning to be absorbed' (2005: 36–37). Audrey Mallet (2016) uncovers a useful article from a 1974 edition of *Unité*. In this piece, Jean-Paul Liégeois interviews some of the extras Costa-Gavras worked with for the scenes of the film shot in Vichy. One of these extras, known as Madame D., still had a positive opinion of Pétain in 1974, maintaining that he had done his best with the hand he was dealt, which was in line with his image as the Shield of France. Madame D. goes on to explain to Liégeois what working as an extra on the film meant to her: 'I gathered some friends together to work on the film … Costa-Gavras's work fascinated us. We don't agree with his ideas but have faith in his attention to detail and the seriousness of his work. If Costa-Gavras has misconceptions, it's because no one has told him the truth' (2016: 265).³ Susan Hayward states that where Villeré faced challenges with his publication in 1972, Costa-Gavras's film production just a few years later would have been more straightforward. She argues: 'By the time Costa-Gavras got to make his film, Valéry Giscard d'Estaing was President, and a new era was launched for cinema in 1974, when censorship was officially abolished' (2020: 22). In relation to the readiness for cultural conversation around historical events, Costa-Gavras flags that for *Special Section*, in particular, his being Greek and Semprún Spanish was raised by numerous interviewers: 'The underlying question, asked in a seemingly naive fashion and simply out of curiosity, was "what does this have to do with you?"' (2018: 270).⁴ The social and historical significance of tackling this period through popular cinema, in spite of controversy or questions of directorial authority, would have been appealing for Costa-Gavras's audience.

In *Special Section*, Costa-Gavras and Semprún connect with contemporary political and cultural concerns. When discussing the proposal to assassinate a German soldier, Costa-Gavras's young activists debate the morality of their methods and of the act of killing itself, thereby engaging audiences with the 1970s debate around left-wing terrorist action. We hear from the group clearly identifiable comments such as:

- This is terrorism, and we've always condemned that. At least let us only kill members of the Gestapo.
- There are workers amongst these soldiers, anti-fascists.
- They might be in their own countries as civilians. But here they are occupation forces.

In comparable scenes, we see how the Minister of Justice and subsequently the judges are convinced that the death penalty for six petty criminals is the correct course of action: the rumoured escalating numbers of German reprisals causes them alarm – 50 then 100 lives saved are rumoured – but mainly, it is the impact on the establishment, and themselves, which prompts them to carry out their acts. Before the communists encounter Moser, their eventual victim, they are shown searching for a suitable German soldier. This includes almost comic scenes of a potential target who wants a photo of himself in Paris, as if he were a mere tourist in the city, and another admiring a young French woman. The inexperienced assassins cannot bring themselves to target these young men who are so like themselves. These moral debates, however, are not the main focus of the film's politics; nor are the young communists, as audiences familiar with Costa-Gavras's work may have expected they would be. The political ire in *Special Section* is directed most strongly at the corruption of the legal system. Costa-Gavras demonstrates this through repetition in the dialogue and through the judges' and lawyers' shocked reactions each time a new person is told of the implementation of the 'retroactive' law. This serves to underscore the seriousness of the procedural changes for an audience who would not be expected to know legal details. It also emphasises that even though the judges were aware of the immorality of their actions, which went against the penal code, for the most part, they still complied. In a televised interview broadcast at the time of *Special Section*'s release, and now accessible online (YouTube), Costa-Gavras explains to Marcel Ophüls, whose *The Sorrow and the Pity (Le Chagrin et la pitié,* 1969) also explored the theme of wartime collaboration, that he has a broader objective in the film: 'It is more about the corruption of justice. Pétainism and Collaboration are the background of the movie'. When pressed by Ophüls, he explains that by this he means the corruption of justice 'in France, and quite everywhere'. Costa-Gavras's intention here aligns with Andy Willis's reading of *Z* (1969), as discussed earlier in this dossier. For audiences of *Special Section*, however, the specificity of the film within its Vichy regime setting problematises the realisation of the director's intention somewhat. The film's epilogue, which states that no sanctions had been made against the judges involved in the special courts, allows Costa-Gavras to provide a more direct comment, with contemporary relevance and standing as a warning for the future. *Special Section* is effective as a political drama, though its placement within the Costa-Gavras and Semprún thriller model is less straightforward.

There were some elements of the film that presented more of a challenge to audiences. One of the clearest deviations from Costa-Gavras's popular previous work, and one which comes from the source material, is the sheer number of characters we see in *Special Section*. Whereas previously Costa-Gavras had successfully used well-known actors to play charismatic lead figures, with this film, there are many characters whom he presents as having equal importance, and therefore the film can be seen to be more fragmented. This fragmentation reflects the content of the book. In the same way that the young activists are not the focus of the film, nor are the six prisoners. The Special Section's woefully arbitrary process that sees the six men put to trial is presented critically, and it is this process that is central to the film. Even though the characters are sometimes presented as snapshots, Costa-Gavras does this with more sensitivity than some critics, such as Vincent Canby of *The New York Times*, saw in the film: 'Aside from the Minister of the Interior (Michel Lonsdale) and the aging Minister of Justice (Louis Seigner) there are scarcely any characters on the screen long enough to register anything except a political position. The movie becomes a series of conference room and corridor and courtroom confrontations' (1975). Canby's observation about the importance and role of setting is accurate. The Grand Casino-Opéra and the Palais de Justice become symbols of the action contained within, and the filming styles and oppressive *mise en scène* reflect this. Indeed, Costa-Gavras also uses similar room-bound and dialogue-driven filming techniques to detail the machinations of European Union decision-making in his 2019 film *Adults in the Room*. This gripping political procedural is also an adaptation of a factual book, in this case, the memoirs of former Greek Finance Minister Yanis Varoufakis. *Special Section* is not the emotionally distant film that some critics suggested. The audience can glean sufficient details in order to understand the characters, and flashback sequences of the prisoners' former lives, for example, assist greatly with this. These sequences contain details from Villeré's original text, and as they are not set in the filmic present, they are freed from the restrictions of the official buildings and have a more light-hearted tone as well as music that matches the change of pace from the fixed camerawork of the court scenes. It is moments such as these that Roy Stafford feels involve the audience in the political stories. For him, Costa-Gavras 'doesn't attempt to use avant-garde techniques to expose those stories/issues. Instead, he allows audiences to find them through his skilfully presented but conventional narratives' (2017).

Semprún and Costa-Gavras have both noted concepts rather than people as the film's main protagonists: Michalczyk quotes press notes, in which Semprún states that the 'deliberate obliteration of traditional plot and heroes' meant Costa-Gavras could 'trace ... the portrait of one of the most terrifying characters known to the twentieth Century: the totalitarian State' (1984: 195).[5] Costa-Gavras's artistic statement in the same document is short and summarised by his intention to explore the 'relationships between man and power' (1975, Cannes document). He later writes that the unusual central character in *Special Section* was 'une loi, inique et illicite' ('an unfair and illegal law') (2018: 266). When discussing the lack of a central protagonist, Michalczyk notes: 'The closest we come to an earlier image of a protagonist is Lucien Sampaix and young Lafarge, but both only appear in the last several sequences of the film' (1984: 201). I agree that if *Special Section* were made as a more typical Costa-Gavras thriller, then journalist Sampaix (Bruno Cremer) or lawyer Lafarge (Jacques Perrin) would be the most appealing choices for a leading actor. It is certainly possible to envisage a film with an expanded part for either character. However, with the model of adhering strictly to the source material and for this particular topic, no one person's testimony can be the most important. Each activist has a role in the course of events, each prisoner's story is important and all of the judges are culpable. Crucially, Pétain is not on screen; we only hear his voice and feel his influence. The actions and procedures portrayed on screen cannot be ascribed to one leader; there is wider, societal responsibility.

A side effect of this different approach to characterisation is that not only do we lack a singular main character but we also then feel the lack of a star. As Hayward details, 'Without a central individual protagonist with a human face (preferably Montand's) vying against the state, the process of subject/audience identification ... became more fraught – indeed, it did not occur'

(1993: 269). The film does feature many well-known French actors who had worked with Costa-Gavras before, such as Perrin and Jean Bouise, the latter being for Smith 'the most persistent face of the *série-Z*' (2005: 41). The director notes that Perrin suggested Louis Seigner for the role of the Minister of Justice, something Costa-Gavras was advised against on the ground of the actor being too '*Comédie-Française*'. However, they went ahead and also chose a number of other actors not known for serious roles such as comic actor Michel Galabiu and Claude Piéplu (*The Discreet Charm of the Bourgeoisie*, 1972) as the President of the Special Section (Costa-Gavras, 2018: 267–68). Costa-Gavras also notes that his friend and fellow left-wing thinker Éric Rouleau, who was not an actor but a journalist – and later an ambassador under François Mitterrand – was given the role of Bernard Friedmann, one of the men being retried. Costa-Gavras's usual star Yves Montand does briefly appear alongside the director and a third man as a customer in a café. This fleeting cameo was written into the film for Montand (Costa-Gavras, 2018: 268), and as it is uncredited, it appears to be more for the actor's solidarity to Costa-Gavras than for marketing the film star's appearance.

As discussed, it was Costa-Gavras and Semprún's intention to stick to the historical events in their film, and they keep to the actions of the key seven days of the story. Until the epilogue, the film presents only what would have been known in 1941 and does not go into the future. For example, Costa-Gavras does not include information about the fate of the family of one of the retried Jewish men (Abraham Trzebrucki) as the book does (Villeré, 1973: 28). And, of course, the audience would bring their own knowledge and experience of World War II to the film. Costa-Gavras does not directly transpose all of the book to the screen; such a vast and detailed adaptation would be challenging for a dramatic film and would stretch too far the bounds of a political thriller.

Costa-Gavras begins and ends the action of the film with precisely constructed scenes in the Vichy Grand Casino-Opéra, where on 10 July 1940, Marshal Pétain had been awarded full power over the new French state. As well as introducing some of the key players in the film, the opening sequence provides a microcosm of Vichy, and the shifting camera position gives the audience a range of points of view, representing the people who embody the ideology of Vichy France, showing the new power structures and hinting at some opposition to the regime. This dramatic introduction to Vichy acts as a primer about the politics of the time and includes: excerpts from Marshal Pétain's famous address from the opera house to the French people; a focus on the American ambassador – significant, in global political terms, by his mere presence in Vichy; a woman succinctly explaining the safety of Vichy during World War II to a child – 'Family' ('*Famille*') being one of the three tenets of Vichy in its tripartite slogan, the others being 'Work' ('*Travail*') and 'Homeland' ('*Patrie*'); a focus on members of the Catholic Church – the camera drawing the audience to the Cardinals' red robes amongst the opera-goers' formal black ties. Following this, religion is not a significant theme in the film, though a priest's cassock provides a disguise for one of the young assassins, and this inclusion in the opera house is an economical reminder to audiences of the close ties between Vichy and the Church. Costa-Gavras would go on to address the relationship between the Catholic Church and Nazism in detail in *Amen* (2002), which itself was controversial in France when released. In this opening scene, the onstage actors' attitude towards Pétain's speech, which their gestures and facial expressions show is negative, is a hint at resistance amongst the theatre company. Costa-Gavras provides the audience with a raft of contextualising information and symbolism in the opening, more than detailed in this summary, and so much so that it warrants multiple viewings. This opening, whilst cinematically interesting and compelling, is not an expected opening for a thriller.

With his cycle of political thrillers, Costa-Gavras had been instrumental in driving major change in popular cinema, combining social and political engagement with genre films. *Special Section* operates as a political drama, using features of the thriller, arguably moving away from popular cinema and manifesting a significant stylistic departure for Costa-Gavras and Semprún.

Notes

1 My translation. Original French: 'Brustlein, encore fasciné par l'événement, n'avait pas bougé. Il restait immobile, figé, revolver au poing, quand il entendit des cris: "Arrêtez-le, arrêtez-le", et en se

retournant il aperçut Fredo. Celui-ci avait déjà remis dans sa poche son revolver et il se ruait vers l'escalier de la sortie'.
2 My translation. Original French: 'j'avais cherché à comprendre et à m'imprégner des situations, de la psychologie des hommes et de leurs conduite. Tous ces fantômes du passé, compagnons de cette passion qu'est l'écriture d'un film, n'avait pas cessé de me hanter'.
3 My translation. Original French: 'Pour le film, j'ai recruté des amis … Le travail de Costa-Gavras nous a passionnés. Nous ne sommes pas d'accord avec ses idées, mais son souci du détail et le sérieux de son travail sont des garanties. Vous savez, si Costa-Gavras a des idées fausses, c'est parce qu'on ne lui a pas dit la vérité'. Original article in Unité can be found at: https://archives-socialistes.fr/app/photopro.sk/archives/detail?docid=32822.
4 My translation. Original French: 'La question qui restait en suspens, comme si elle avait été posée naïvement et par simple curiosité, était: "De quoi vous mêlez-vous?"'.
5 United Artists' *Special Section* press notes are available in full at: http://galateefilms.com/wp-content/uploads/2017/12/special-section.pdf.

References

Canby, V. (1975, 12 August). 'Screen: 'Special Section' by Costa-Gavras Arrives'. *New York Times*. Retrieved from: www.nytimes.com/1975/12/08/archives/screen-special-section-by-costagavras-arrives-frenchmen-collaborate.html

Costa-Gavras, C. (2018). *Va où il est impossible d'aller: Mémoires*. Paris: Editions du Seuil.

Hayward, S. (1993). *French National Cinema*. London: Routledge.

Hayward, S. (2020). '*Un homme de trop* (1967) and *Section spéciale* (1975): Justice Unravelled, a Tale of Two Frances (1941 and 1943)'. In H. B. Pettey (Ed.), *The Films of Costa-Gavras: New Perspectives*. Manchester: Manchester University Press.

Liégeois, J. (1974, 22 November). 'Vichy sans chagrin, ni pitié'. *L'Unité*, 133. Retrieved from: https://archives-socialistes.fr/app/photopro.sk/archives/detail?docid=32822

Mallet, A. (2016). 'Vichy against Vichy: History and Memory of the Second World War in the Former Capital of the État français from 1940 to the Present'. Retrieved from: https://core.ac.uk/download/pdf/211519546.pdf

Michalczyk, J. J. (1984). *Costa-Gavras: The Political Fiction Film*. London: Associated University Presses.

Smith, A. (2005). *French Cinema in the 1970s*. Manchester: Manchester University Press.

Stafford, R. (2017). 'Special Section'. Retrieved from: https://itpworld.wordpress.com/?s=special+section

United Artists. *Special Section* Cannes 1975 press notes. Retrieved from: http://galateefilms.com/wp-content/uploads/2017/12/special-section.pdf

Villeré, H. (1973). *L'Affaire de la Section Spéciale*. Paris: Arthème Fayard.

YouTube. *The Political Films of Costa-Gavras: Interview with Marcel Ophüls* [Video file]. Retrieved from: www.youtube.com/watch?v=-Cahm-I4Q9Q

7

The political thriller in the context of Italian cinema

Andy Willis

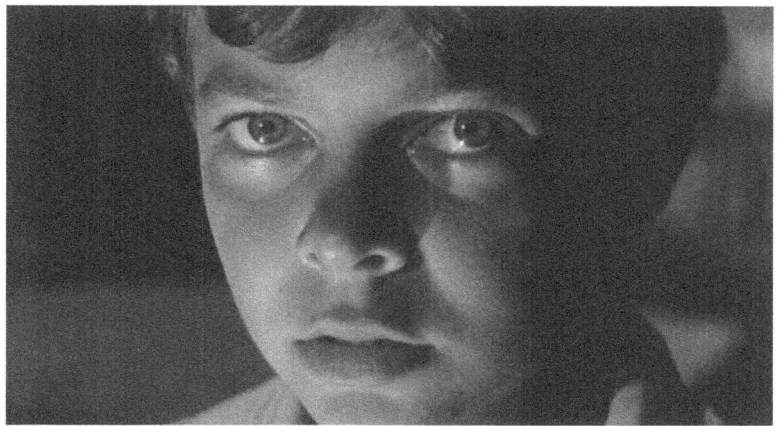

Figure 8 *Don't Torture a Duckling* (1972), courtesy of Arrow Films

As with elsewhere in Europe, in the post-World War II era Italian cinema was one that was very much concerned with politics. By the late 1960s, that had, as elsewhere, taken on a new urgency. A number of directors who had emerged in the 1950s and early 1960s were joined by a younger generation of politicised filmmakers. Together, they produced work that has been collectively labelled 'political film'. Peter Bondanella identified this cycle of political films as a *'filone'* (2009 242). The term *filone* refers to the cycles of production that came to dominate Italian film production in the 1960s. As Mary P. Wood notes, 'A *filone* is a strand of similar films, rather than a genre. Trendspotting successful subjects, names, themes and stars resulted in quickly-made similar films, until public interest waned' (2005: 11). By terming 'the political film' a *filone*, there is a certain acknowledgement that the works that made it up had some impact with audiences, hence encouraging further investment in films that also addressed political subjects. Gaetana Marrone has noted that this film cycle emerged at a particularly charged historical moment, one that was having an impact across other parts of Europe. She states:

> In Italy, the radical filmmaking of the 1960s and 1970s was born during a period of economic and social transformation that accompanied the industrialisation of a country that was prevalently rural. Responding to these new economic and social developments was a group of young directors who had inherited the ethics, political commitment and social awareness of neorealism.
>
> 2014: 194

What is significant is that within this moment of political filmmaking, practitioners chose to work in a variety of styles and genres. These extended from the more auteur projects of Pasolini (*Pigsty* (*Porcile*), 1969, for example) to the literary adaptations of Visconti (*Death in Venice* (*Morte a Venezia*), 1971). Amongst these politically motivated films were a number that embraced popular genres such as the western and the thriller.

In the late 1960s, this political filmmaking responded to the increasing disillusionment with the operations of the Italian state. Once again, some practitioners looked to connect with audiences through adopting film styles that had the potential to reach a wide audience. Many involved in these projects had direct links or were associated with left-wing organisations such as the Communist Party of Italy (PCI). In the post-war era, the PCI had emerged as an advocate and supporter of the developing neorealist film movement within the country. This went hand in hand with an emerging sense of the importance of films in the wider political struggle based on what their role may be in the forging of a sense of nation. As Stephen Gundle has noted, 'For some ten years, starting from the run-up to the first parliamentary elections in 1948, it [the PCI] conducted concerted actions in defence of Italian national cinema. As a result, it won the allegiance of many of the most important film-makers in the country' (2014: 79).

One of the main tenets of the PCI's support for Italian films was a critique of the products of Hollywood. Director Elio Petri, who had been a film critic for *L'Unita*, the daily newspaper of the Communist Party, before becoming a filmmaker, reflected this idea when he stated that 'America was using Hollywood films as propaganda in favour of the American system, presenting the American consumer society as a model' (1983: 54). Petri went on to articulate how as a filmmaker, he attempted to make work that engaged audiences with political ideas. He argued that his work was 'not aimed at convincing those who already have my political and ideological convictions. Rather, it tries through a dialectical process, to reach those who are still outsiders to these ideas' (1983: 56). In order to achieve this, Petri developed a close working collaboration with actor Gian Maria Volonté, who contributed distinctive performances to his *We Still Kill the Old Way* (*A ciascuno il suo*, 1967), *The Working Class Goes to Heaven* (*La classe operaia va in paradiso*, 1971) and *Todo modo* (1976). His presence is perhaps best utilised by Petri in his ultra-stylish *Investigation of a Citizen above Suspicion* (1970), where he plays a police inspector who manipulates the scene of a crime in a manner that ultimately reveals that the police force is not only ineffective but corrupt to the core and worthy of no one's trust. Previously, Volonté had established his popularity with audiences through performances in the likes of westerns *For a Few Dollars More* (*Per qualche dollaro in più*, 1965), *A Bullet for the General* (*Quién sabe?*, 1966) and *Face to Face* (*Faccia a facia*, 1967), as well as developing a reputation for political activism.

Another of the Italian directors who was at one time close to the PCI's sphere of influence was Carlo Lizzani. Having been influential in Roberto Rossellini's connections to the Party in the 1940s and later an important scriptwriter, Lizzani himself would direct two films, *Attention! Bandits!* (*Achtung! Banditi!*, 1951) and *Chronicles of Poor Lovers* (*Cronache di poveri amanti*, 1953), produced by the *Cooperativa Spettatori Produttivi*, an organisation close to the PCI. In a marked shift from the PCI's previous distrust of commercial films based on Hollywood models, and perhaps reflecting his distancing from the Party, in the 1960s, Lizzani would take his political filmmaking into more obviously popular arenas. For example, in the mid-1960s, at the height of the popularity of the *filone*, he made westerns such as *The Hills Run Red* (*Un Fiume di dollari*,

1966) and a notable contribution to the cycle of films set in Mexico and focusing on revolutionary politics with *Requiescant* (1967), the latter a film which contains a small but significant part of an enigmatic peasant revolutionary leader played by another filmmaker familiar with the politics of the PCI, Pier Paolo Pasolini.

In his turn to more commercial subjects, Lizzani also made a number of crime films. These often focused on marginalised groups within Italy's cities, whose turn to crime can be articulated in terms of their seeking to find a place in a society that rejects them. Two of Lizzani's most notable crime films of the 1960s, *Wake Up and Kill* (*Svegliati e uccidi*, 1966) and *Bandits in Milan* (*Banditi a Milano*, 1968), are based on real-life stories of crime. As Marco Paoli points out, the use of the Cavallero gang in the latter 'illustrates the way the new generation of criminals of the immediate post-economic miracle period made a transition from the use of non-violent to violent criminal methods, and took the methods of the capitalist system to a ruthlessly logical conclusion' (2011: 44). In drawing from widely reported recent events, Lizzani adopted an approach that created narratives that were 'ripped from the headlines'. The immediacy of these stories meant that with films such as *Bandits in Milan*, political filmmakers like Lizzani, as Paoli puts it, 'used the crime genre to explore the criminal underside of Italy's economic prosperity and examined real-life events and characters that were emblematic of the darker side of the epoch's acquisitional fervour and wealth accumulation' (2011: 44). He goes on to argue that '*Bandits in Milan* reflects this social trend and emphasizes the evolving behaviour of individuals within criminal contexts as a consequence of Metropolitan neo-gangsterism and the lure of capitalism in the capitalist system, providing thus a controversial social critique' (2011: 44–45). This is the case with *Bandits in Milan* where the criminals' actions, again as Paoli notes, show how politicised individuals and groups:

> Realized that it was impossible to put into effect their political beliefs when society was beginning to gravitate around capitalism, personal success and consumerism, and this disillusionment, together with a belief that there was no adequate political alternative to oppose these values, led to the creation of terrorist groups such as the Red Brigades and their evolution during the so-called years of lead.
> 2011: 51

The ways in which society had changed, and the political consequences of those changes, would become central to a number of the political thrillers that followed in the 1970s.

Responding to the years of lead

Broadly speaking, the *anni di piombo*, or the 'years of lead', began with the Piazza Fontana bombing in Milan in 1969 and would include all the 1970s and into the early 1980s. One of the key things that is associated with the years of lead was the idea of a 'strategy of tension', or *stragismo*. Alan O'Leary suggests that this was 'a campaign to establish a "presidential" or quasi-authoritarian type of political system in Italy by throwing the state into a law-and-order crisis that would make a takeover by the military or far right seem desirable to the Italian populace' (2010: 245). Central to this was the campaign of bombings, such as the one at Bologna station in 1980, undertaken by neo-fascist groups who were widely thought to be protected by the Italian state intelligence services. As a response to this, some on the left moved in the direction of violence themselves and from this emerged groups such as the *Brigate Rosse* (Red Brigades) and the later *Prima Linea* (Front Line). As O'Leary notes, for them:

> 'Armed struggle' translated into the kidnapping, knee-capping, and eventually assassination of policemen, journalists, judges, politicians and businessmen. The most notorious action of left-wing terrorism was the kidnap of politician Aldo Moro by the BR in 1978. His five bodyguards were murdered and he himself was killed after 54 days of captivity.
>
> 2010: 245

As discussed by Ellen Smith in her consideration of *Investigation of a Citizen above Suspicion* (1970) in this volume, the strategy of tension, and the complex webs of corruption it implied, would become the background for some of the key political thrillers of the period. Again, as Alan O'Leary notes, some of the most immediate responses to the years of lead occurred in the more popular corners of Italian cinema. He states that 'For much of the 1970s it was not the culturally valued, politically committed or auteurist cinema that addressed the problem or phenomenon of terrorism but the genres of the cop film (the *poliziesco*) and the so-called Italian-style comedy (*commedia all'italiana*)' (2010: 245). Amongst these, images of terrorism occurred in a number of Italian political thrillers of the 1970s. What is significant is the fact that these cinematic responses were being produced at a time when the events were still an ongoing threat in society.

Within the realm of the thriller, the *filone* of the *poliziottesco* (as Austin Fisher terms it), or police procedural, proved particularly popular. Fisher notes that the term became associated more broadly with the Italian crime film of the 1970s, encompassing 'mafia, heist and vigilante narratives' (2019: 43). O'Leary posits 1972's *The Law Enforcers* (*La polizia ringrazia*) directed by Stefano Vanzina, which he observes 'contains a representation of right-wing vigilantism and of a subversive plan for an authoritarian takeover of the state', as the initiator of this particular *filone* (2010: 245). Fisher goes on to distinguish these lower-budget, more rapidly produced films from the political films of Rosi, Petri and Damiani. One of the major distinctions was the level of engagement with the complexities of Italian politics of the 1970s. He notes that a number of these films 'sought directly to portray high-profile terrorism and official cover-ups of the era', whilst others 'depict the unmasking of official culpability behind acts of terror' (2019: 9).

What is particularly interesting about a range of these films, such as the example of *Killer Cop* (*La polizia ha le mani legate*, 1975) discussed in this dossier by MaoHui Deng, is how they take the context of a highly charged political and social Italy and use it more or less simply as a backdrop for their conspiracy thriller. Unlike directors such as Damiani, with *Killer Cop*, Luciano Ercoli seems less interested in exploring the detail of the politics that informs the story and more interested in the macho posturing of his lead character. As Fisher puts it, with regard to an engagement with the politics of the setting, such films 'seek, not to explain or to "make sense" of the events, but instead to enact a ritual recognition of only partially understood, but pervasive and therefore assumed, corruption' (2019: 11). These more popular engagements with the political thriller in the form of the *poliziottesco* reveal how far political content had become embedded within Italian films.

Writer Leonardo Sciascia would prove to be a significant contributor to the political thrillers that engaged with the years of lead as a number of important films from the period were adapted from his novels. After writing a number of works that engaged in political commentary, in the 1970s, Sciascia's political commitment would see him become a member of the Palermo town council when, in 1975, he was elected as an independent candidate on the list put forward by the PCI. He served in that role until 1977 when he began to distance himself from the PCI due to his opposition to their dealings with the Christian Democratic Party (*Democrazia Cristiana*). Following this, Sciascia would go on to gain election to both the Italian Parliament and to the European Parliament as a candidate for the left-wing Italian Radical Party (*Partito Radicale Italiano*). Taking office in 1979, his period as a Deputy came to an end in 1983 with the dissolution of Parliament.

Sciascia's writing was noted for taking the form of the detective story and using it to offer investigations into contemporary social and political concerns. As Jo-Ann Cannon argues, 'The detective genre perfectly captures Sciascia's *forma mentis*. His work is situated between two poles, belief in the exercise of reason as symbolized in the *giallo* (detective novel) and dismay at the defeat of reason and the prevalence of injustice in the world' (2006: 4). In 1961, he had published *Il giorno della civetta* (*Day of the Owl*), a novel that explored the power and influence of the mafia on Sicilian society and politics. In 1968, Damiano Damiani directed a film adaptation of the novel starring Franco Nero which proved successful at the box office and showed an appetite amongst audiences for political work. Before the release of Damiani's *Day of the Owl*, Sciascia's 1966 novel *A ciascuno il suo* (*To Each His Own*) had been adapted by Elio Petri and his regular screenwriting collaborator Ugo Pirro for their 1967 film *We Still Kill in the Old Way* (*A ciascuno il suo*). In 1971, Sciascia published *Il contesto* (*Equal Danger*), another political detective novel which was adapted by Francesco Rosi, Tonino Guerra and Lino Iannuzzi for the 1976 film *Illustrious Corpses* (*Cadaveri eccellenti*), one of the most critically acclaimed films of the period. Sciascia would publish another politically driven novel, *Todo modo*, about the links between the Christian Democrats and the Catholic Church in 1974. This was adapted into a film of the same name, once again by Elio Petri, in 1976.

It is perhaps not surprising that the directors of the adaptations of Sciascia's novels were themselves some of the most high-profile left-leaning filmmakers. As Cannon further suggests, 'In his early detective novels, whether set in Sicily or in unnamed countries that bear a striking resemblance to Italy, Sciascia targets both the Sicilian mafia and the larger mafia of power politics in Italy' (2006: 5). It is this aspect of his work that proved appealing to political filmmakers who saw in his investigative novel the opportunity to make films that were able to draw on the codes and conventions of the thriller to create politically motivated investigative films.

Before the 1970s, Francesco Rosi had already built an international reputation based on a series of politicised films that explored corruption within Italian society. These included *Salvatore Giuliano* (1962) and *Hands over the City* (*Le mani sulla città*, 1963) and introduced a style that was centred on characters undertaking investigations – often exposing political corruption – and utilised flashbacks at key points to reveal crucial events. Like Costa-Gavras, Rosi enjoyed a series of close collaborations, and all three films starred Gian Maria Volonté, were shot by cinematographer Pasqualino De Santis and enjoyed script collaboration from Tonino Guerra. The trio are also marked by a clear desire to place characters in social and political contexts and use that as a way of exploring corruption and power relations rather than simply telling the story of individuals. To this end, Rosi's adoption of an investigative narrative model invited his audiences to ask questions and engage with the issues explored on screen as the film progressed and come to an understanding of how power can be manipulated and abused.

The 1970s would see Rosi make a series of films that developed a style that might be best described as 'investigative thriller'. In succession, he directed three important works, *The Mattei Affair* (*Il Caso Mattei*, 1972), *Lucky Luciano* (1974) and *Illustrious Corpses* (*Cadaveri Eccellenti*, 1976), that all further honed this technique to offer critiques of the establishment within Italy and explore the reasons why the 1970s became a decade where the trust in government was eroded to such an extent that elements of both the left and right took up arms.

Winner of the *Palme D'Or* at the Cannes Film Festival, *The Mattei Affair* is an ambitious work offering both an investigation into the death of industrialist Enrico Mattei and images of Rosi and his collaborators working on the film. The latter aspect was inspired by the disappearance (and presumed death) of Mauro De Mauro. Known as the 'inconvenient journalist' due to his investigative reporting, De Mauro worked for the Palermo-based newspaper *L'Ora* and had been undertaking some research for Rosi's project before he vanished. Ultimately, *The Mattei Affair* is a challenging film that asks audiences to think about the complex links between international business interests, organised crime and political corruption. Another of Rosi's frequent collaborators, the actor Gian Maria Volonté, gives an impressive, committed performance as Mattei and would go on to play another key role for Rosi in his next political drama, *Lucky Luciano*.

Lucky Luciano is an ambitious film that once again explores the international links between organised crime, politicians and big business. Here, that focuses on the influence of the Mafia on both sides of the Atlantic. Avoiding many of the violent trappings of the genre of the gangster film, *Lucky Luciano* privileges Rosi's desire to expose the ways in which criminality is intertwined in a number of society's institutions and how global economic networks assist in the expansion and sustenance of such corruption. According to *The Guardian*'s obituary for the director, novelist Norman Mailer called *Lucky Luciano* 'the finest movie yet made about the mafia, the most thoughtful, the truest and most sensitive to the paradoxes of a society of crime' (Robinson and Lane, 2015).

Illustrious Corpses shows an Italy rife with mistrust and paranoia. The story follows a detective as he investigates the deaths of a number of high-profile judges. Lino Ventura's quietly effective detective is appointed to investigate who is responsible and soon begins to unearth an array of corruption and duplicity within the corridors of power. Highly atmospheric, this is perhaps the archetypal political film of the 1970s and displays to great effect Rosi's sophisticated visual style and use of sound. As Salvatore Bizzarro argues, 'the force of the film lies in the tension it creates; the more the tension grows, the better it transmits the filmmaker's direction' (1996: 103).

With *Illustrious Corpses*, as Alan O'Leary argues:

> Rosi shows Italian democracy to have already been compromised by corruption, by state collusion with the mafia, and by the oppressive presence of surveillance (the latter is expressed in passages of great formal brilliance including a highly unusual sound design). *Cadaveri*

eccellenti portrays Italian society as a kind of panoptical prison from which escape is impossible and in which political opposition is a convenient pretext for repression.

2010: 246

In terms of Italian directors who tackled the subject of Mafia-driven corruption within the political and social structures of the country in the form of the political thriller, one of the most noted was Damiano Damiani. Today best remembered for the political western *Bullet for the General* (1966), the director made a series of thrillers in the late 1960s and 1970s that explored corruption within Italy's political institutions and their involvement with the Mafia. His 1968 adaptation of Leonardo Sciascia's novel *Day of the Owl* is perhaps his most well-known political thriller, and the film directly exposed the collaboration of local politicians and the Mafia, to such an extent that the production was threatened when shooting in Sicily. His other work included *Confessions of a Police Captain* (1971), which focused on corruption within the police force, and *How to Kill a Judge* (1975), which extended its critique to include the potential negative influence of the media on society.

The form of the murder mystery thriller also offered filmmakers the opportunity to explore politics in a less literal, and more popular, manner than employed by the likes of Rosi, Petri or Damiani. In the late 1960s and early 1970s, the Italian industry produced a series of dark, heavily stylised murder mysteries known collectively as the *gialli*. The *gialli* is a popular style of Italian films that often utilizes a 'whodunnit' plot and is named after the yellow covers that marked out the popular, often pulp, crime fiction that had been published by Mondadori since the late 1920s. *Giallo* films, which emerged in the 1960s, began to incorporate violent murders that, in the 1970s, became increasingly imaginative in their visual and aural construction. These striking sequences began to pepper the narratives of the *gialli* like the song and dance numbers in musicals. Some accused the 1970s *giallo* films of being misogynistic due to the way that the predominantly female victims were killed with cinematic relish. The *gialli* found real success at the box office with *The Bird with the Crystal Plumage* (*L'uccello dalle piume di cristallo*, Dario Argento, 1970), and this hit was followed by a slew of avian- and animal-influenced titles looking to cash in on its success. One of these was

Lucio Fulci's 1972 *Don't Torture a Duckling* (*Non si sevizia un paperino*), a film that took the *giallo* format and used it to create a meditation on the corrupting influence of the Catholic Church and its morality on Italy's rural south. Fulci's work is a great example of the ways in which a popular form, here the *giallo* style of violent thriller, could be used to critique society's institutions, and it is in films such as this that the form moves close to that of the political thriller. Set in rural Italy, *Don't Torture a Duckling* focuses on a series of brutal murders where the killer seems to target young boys on the verge of adulthood. As the media flocks to the village where the victims lived, suspicion falls on those residents who, due to their lifestyles, are considered outsiders. This rural setting had already proved an effective backdrop for a discussion of political corruption in *Day of the Owl*. Rumour has persisted that Fulci was subsequently blacklisted due to his critical representation of Italy's powerful social institutions.

The variety of filmmakers and styles that embraced the politics of the era suggests that there is much more to uncover about Italian popular films than simply the thrillers. On reflection, one could argue that the idea of an Italian political thriller bled into a range of *filone* rather than being an exclusive category in itself, as the *serie-Z* had become in France. From the prestige auteur productions of Rosi and Petri to the middle-brow thrillers of Damiani and the more pulp work of genre stalwarts such as Fulci, the political thriller was a significant response to a pressing social and political context. The case studies that follow attempt to assess two key titles from across the different manifestations of the political thriller in Italian cinema of the 1970s.

References

Bizzarro, S. (1996). 'Dancing with Corpses: Murder, Politics and Power in Illustrious Corpses'. In C. Testa (Ed.), *Poet of Civic Courage: The Films of Francesco Rosi*. Westport: Praeger, 101–115.
Bondanella, P. (2009). *A History of Italian Cinema*. London: Continuum.
Cannon, J. (2006). *The Novel as Investigation: Leonardo Sciascia, Dacia Maraini, and Antonio Tabucchi*. Toronto: University of Toronto Press.
Fisher, A. (2019). *Blood in the Streets: Histories of Violence in Italian Crime Cinema*. Edinburgh: Edinburgh University Press.

Gundle, S. (2014). 'Neorealism and Left-Wing Culture'. In P. Bondanella (Ed.), *The Italian Cinema Book*. London: BFI, 77–83.
Marrone, G. (2014). 'The Political Film'. In P. Bondanella (Ed.), *The Italian Cinema Book*. London: BFI, 195–202.
O'Leary, A. (2010). 'Italian Cinema and the "anni di piombo" '. *Journal of European Studies*, 40(3), 243–257.
Paoli, M. (2011). 'Metropolitan Neo-Gangsterism and the Lure of Capitalism in Carlo Lizzani's Bandits in Milan'. *Studies in European Cinema*, 8(1), 43–55.
Petri, E. (1983). 'Cinema Is Not for the Elite, but for the Masses'. In D. Georgakas and L. Rubenstein (Eds), *The Cineaste Interviews: On the Art and Politics of the Cinema*. Chicago: Lake View Press, 87–97.
Robinson, D. and Lane, J. F. (2015). 'Francesco Rosi Obituary'. *The Guardian*. Retrieved from: www.theguardian.com/film/2015/jan/11/francesco-rosi
Wood, M. P. (2005). *Italian Cinema*. Oxford: Berg.

8

Investigation of a Citizen above Suspicion (*Indagine su un cittadino al di sopra di ogni sospetto*), Elio Petri, 1970

Ellen Smith

Figure 9 *Investigation of a Citizen above Suspicion* (1970), courtesy of Park Circus/Criterion

Investigation of a Citizen above Suspicion, released in 1970, is the most celebrated work of Italian filmmaker Elio Petri and a significant entry into Europe's political thrillers from the decade. It takes a sardonic look at the fascist practices of Italy's law enforcement in the late 1960s, following a high-ranking homicide police inspector (played by *States of Danger and Deceit* favourite Gian Maria Volonté) who murders his mistress and then watches his own department fail to suspect him, despite his leaving glaring clues pointing towards his guilt. His goal in doing this is not to expose the incompetence of the police and the unjust failings of the law but rather to reinforce his own fascistic fixation with authority to prove that his rank and strength of personality grants him complete legal immunity and unrestrained corruption of power. In his words, it is his 'sacrifice' with which he hopes to 'reaffirm, in all its purity, the concept of authority'.

Petri is a filmmaker closely associated with Italy's cinematic output during its historic *anni di piombo* (years of lead) of the 1970s and 1980s. Like the other left-leaning Italian directors of the period, he responded to the social turmoil of this era by fusing filmmaking with political analysis, contributing to the celebrated canon of *film d'inchiesta* (cine-investigations) in the 1960s and 1970s. Petri's leftist inclination was apparent from an early age, influenced by his working-class upbringing and an affiliation with the Italian Communist Party in his youth. After writing film criticism for the Party's newspapers, he became an assistant director, most notably to Giuseppe De Santis (*Bitter Rice*, 1949, and *Rome 11:00*, 1952), and then a scriptwriter, learning his craft during the post-war era of Italian neorealist cinema. Though the films of this period were infused with social and political themes, Petri found the school of neorealism to be preoccupied with economic determinism, whilst Italy was entering the new era of its transformative 'economic miracle' post-1958. He started to make his own films in which he could explore Italy's new economic terrain whilst rejecting the deterministic conventions of neorealism, instead presenting the psychology of the individual as a site of political action and existential struggle. As he put it in 1962, 'The themes that come to our attention today are all internal. The protagonist of *Ladri di biciclette* [*Bicycle Thieves*, 1948] today must face not only the society in which he lives in but also his own conscience' (Gili, 2013: 104).

Having left the Italian Communist Party in 1956 after the Soviet intervention in Hungary, Petri reconciled with Marxism after becoming a director, particularly the trend of 'existential Marxism' which fused the ideas of Marx and Freud and had been made popular by philosophers like Jean-Paul Sartre. The representation of personal subjectivities as a means to critique the social consciousness at large is perhaps the most recognisable characteristic of Petri's work, particularly as his films became more historically precise as Europe's (and particularly Italy's) political situation grew increasingly agitated. The individual subjects who come under interrogation are always Italian men (often played by Gian Maria Volonté), both blue-collar workers, such as *The Working Class Go to Heaven*'s (*La classe operaia va in paradiso*, 1971) factory worker Lulu, and men of institutional power, such as *Investigation of a Citizen above Suspicion*'s inspector and *Todo modo*'s (1976) Christian Democratic leader 'M', based on real party leader Aldo Moro. These individuals are psychologically unravelled in Petri's strange, contradictory worlds, which are often cruel yet darkly comic. In many ways, Petri's cinema can be considered a cinema of contradictions, one that is sometimes at odds in style and jarring in tone but perfectly matched to the director's neurotic characters and cynical world view. Williams (2013) also identifies this characteristic: 'For Petri, a world of irresolvable contradiction deserved a contradictory cinema.'

Petri's representation of the inspector's neurosis in *Investigation of a Citizen above Suspicion* gives the titular 'Investigation' a triple meaning: it is the police's futile investigation into a murder whose culprit is immune to the law, an investigation by the inspector into how far he can push his immunity and, most importantly, Petri's investigation into his lead character's psyche. The inspector is played with a brutish and frantic temperament by Volonté, whose performance might bring something to mind like Christian Bale's Patrick Bateman in *American Psycho* (Mary Harron, 2000) for modern audiences. But for the mainstream European audience in 1970, Volonté's performance would have undeniably felt like an evocation of Mussolini, particularly in the scene where the inspector gives an impassioned address to his department in which he calls for the end of subversion and revolution, finishing with the Freudian quote 'Repression is civilization!'

Investigation of a Citizen above Suspicion would become the first part in Petri and screenwriter Ugo Pirro's 'Trilogy of Neurosis', where the themes of power, work and money are explored respectively in an increasingly eccentric manner. The second instalment in the trilogy, *The Working Class Go to Heaven* (*La classe operaia va *in paradiso*, released in the US as *Lulu the Tool*) from 1971 follows a disillusioned factory worker navigating labour relations, whilst the third part, *Property Is No Longer a Theft* (*La proprietà non é più un furto*) from 1973, presents a Marxist bank clerk who is literally allergic to money and tormented by humanity's fixation with it. Petri's unification of these socially and economically varied figures (the labourer, the Marxist bank worker, the fascist law enforcement officer) through a triptych of shared neurosis can be read as a comment on the extent of capitalism's powerful hold on Italian society and the alienation it engenders. After Italy's post-war economic boom, Petri seems to view capital and social order as so ingrained into the everyday psychology of most Italian citizens that if people are to challenge the order of things, no matter what their position, they also put their sanity at risk.

Investigation of a Citizen above Suspicion's inspector is afflicted with the neurosis of power, or what he calls the inevitable 'occupational disease' of a prolonged time in authority. It is the impossibility of failure in his experiment that begins to torment him, never remorse for his victim, which then catalyses an existential crisis when he is ultimately confronted with a life without consequences. In this way, *Investigation of a Citizen above Suspicion* is often described as Kafkaesque because of its absurd representation of bureaucratic procedures and a character who is undone in the face of them. The film explicitly references Kafka by ending on a synoptic quote from his 1925 novel *The Trial*: 'Whatever he may seem to us, he is yet a servant of the Law; that is, he belongs to the Law and as such is set beyond human judgment.'

In Petri's films, a fractured psyche also means a fractured formal style, and the worsening psychological breakdown of *Investigation of a Citizen above Suspicion*'s lead is communicated through the film's visual and aural expressionism. The camerawork, by Petri's regular cinematographer Luigi Kuveiller, is often handheld and restless, pressing near to the faces of the actors and frequently so close to Volonté that the audience can see the paranoid sweat collecting on his face. Objects are also often positioned noticeably close to the lens of the camera, transforming them into abstract blurry shapes that obscure our view and heighten the sense of unease, whilst reflective surfaces and lines are utilised to visually denote the inspector's split public and private persona. The most fractured aspect of *Investigation of a Citizen above Suspicion* is its shifting tone, which is absurdly comedic at times but evolves into something more sobering and historically exact. The comic-sinister score, composed by Ennio Morricone, further reflects this, providing a jaunty motif that matches the inspector's initially playful attitude towards his crime but one that feels equally jarring and misplaced next to the film's moments of brutality and realism. This is all evidence of Petri's 'contradictory' approach and the filmic embodiment of an individual whose initially irreverent experiment transforms into full-blown existential nightmare.

Williams (2013) also acknowledges Petri's contradicting stylistic choices and notes the director's frequent borrowing from various genres, stating:

> Petri made strange from within a number of recognizable genre schemata, from *giallo* to sci-fi to the Mafia film and the police procedural. And while some critics have seen this as the absence of a coherent style, it's more productive to understand these generic frames as a set of interference patterns and frictions that give the films' antipathy to modern life something meaty to sink their jagged teeth into.

Investigation of a Citizen above Suspicion is almost an amalgamation of some of these genres, with its *giallo*-esque scenes of sexual transgression and violence, use of dark comedy and, most importantly, its elements of the thriller. Though, in staying true to his contradictory style, any genre signifiers that Petri sets up are quickly subverted, and this is where *Investigation of a Citizen above Suspicion* may be considered a 'contradictory' thriller of sorts, particularly in the way it complicates the sense of tension. For example, one of the defining elements of *giallo*-style thrillers is the concealment of the culprit right up until the final act, yet here, Petri swiftly reveals the killer in the opening moments of the film. Tension is instead generated from the inspector's game-playing with his department and the audience's uncertainty of whether he will be suspected and caught, yet the probability of this becomes more and more unlikely as the extent of the corruption is revealed. The film's ending does not bring satisfying resolution nor retribution for its killer but rather an absurdly business-as-usual approach to the inspector's confession, as he is proven to be truly above suspicion.

Investigation of a Citizen above Suspicion may begin as a thriller but as the initial tension fades and the inspector's fate is sealed, it ends as more of a procedural, Kafkaesque parable. As Petri makes this shift, a harsh representation of reality in Italy in the late 1960s emerges. The year of the film's release, 1970, was within one of the most politically fraught decades for Italy and Europe and an appropriate moment for filmmakers to openly criticise corruption within law enforcement, following on as it did from recent protests and demonstrations in the late 1960s around which the conduct of the police towards young revolutionaries had become highly controversial. The middle section of the film sees the inspector and his colleagues mercilessly shifting the blame for the murder between the gay husband of the victim (Massimo Foschi) and anarchist student Antonio Pace (Sergio Tramonti). The lawmen talk openly about their far-reaching surveillance of these convenient suspects and problematic radicals, and even long before we are aware of his plans to frame Pace, the inspector asks 'Is his line tapped?', to which his colleague (Vittorio Duse) responds with a pointedly political 'Of course, chief. Since May 1968.' These surveillance methods were all very real, tried and tested techniques used by 1960s and 1970s Italian police, whose objective was to covertly survey criminal activity which could then be used to frame leftist radicals and engender fear. This became referred to as a 'strategy of tension' (*strategia della tensione*) during the years of lead, in other words, the creation of tension as a means to reaffirm the need for social order under authoritarian governance. Whilst the filming of *Investigation of a Citizen above Suspicion* had already finished before the 1969 Milan Piazza Fontana bombing, its release shortly thereafter would have felt inextricably linked to this event for Italian audiences in the 1970s, who had lived through its devastation. This was a terrorist attack in which seventeen people were killed and eighty-eight injured, perpetrated by the right-wing group *Ordine Nuovo* ('New Order') but also initially blamed on leftwing anarchists. In 1970, Elio Petri would go on to make a documentary about one of the most infamous falsely accused radicals, Giuseppe Pinelli, who died suspiciously by falling from the fourth-floor window of Milan's central police station whilst being detained for questioning about the bombing.

Despite these fraught circumstances, *Investigation of a Citizen above Suspicion* was granted an uncensored theatrical release and the film went on to wide international acclaim, buoyed by the increasingly prevalent mistrust of authoritative power around Europe. The film's premiere predictably incited upset from Italian law enforcement, but it also didn't go without some criticism from various leftist newspaper critics, film journals, trade unions and extra-parliamentary leftist groups of the time. Their problem was mainly with Petri's use of dark humour and absurdity, as some felt the film's caricatural tendencies were treating very real matters with an overly constructed, comic approach and therefore any real criticism was lost. Others on the left took issue with the scenes inside police detainment rooms, where the lawmen's dialogue implies an inevitable factionalism amongst the young leftists. After hearing the imprisoned activists arguing in their cells, the commissioner says 'As long as they fight among themselves, we will have no problem', whilst another officer jokes 'After two hours, they've already split up into four groups.' The idea that the radicals in the film are an essential or even complicit counterpart to their oppressors was beyond the pale for many leftists of the time (Portis, 2010: 44). Dismissal from those on the left would extend to the entirety of Petri's 'Trilogy of Neurosis', and the consensus was that Petri's work was 'an unwarranted individualization of a revolutionary consciousness reduced to a mere psychological or existential matter' (Resmini, 2018: 73); in other words, they found Petri's 'psychoanalysis' of individual subjects to be dismissive of the collective struggle and antithetical to Marxist praxis. One of the most memorable leftist critiques of Petri's work would come from French Marxist filmmaker Jean-Marie Straub, who, after the film's 1971 Paris premiere, declared that every copy of *The Working Class Go to Heaven* ought to be burned. Unscathed, Petri followed the 'Trilogy of Neurosis' with the even more idiosyncratic *Todo modo*.

Further retrospective criticism of *Investigation of a Citizen above Suspicion* has focused on the film's treatment of Augusta Terzi, the inspector's mistress played by Florinda Bolkan, who is murdered in an act of sexual violence in the very first scene of the film. The women of Petri's worlds are complex but remain permanently on the periphery, usually as wives, lovers, mistresses and mothers. Terzi is no exception; she is given little to say and is only seen in the sexualised context of the film's flashbacks after she is killed. However, these scenes also add another crucial layer to Petri's critique. Interestingly, we learn Terzi shared the inspector's masochistic sexual desires but grew tired of his bureaucratic appearance and sexual weakness and is seen berating him for reminding her of a child. Terzi dares to challenge the inspector and take on a more dominant role, and the inspector responds by slashing her throat during their final sexual encounter, a vitriolic attempt at reclaiming both his authoritative and sexual power. In these moments, the character of the inspector resembles the remnants of the 'New Italian' from the country's years under fascism, where aggression and virility were deemed the most important characteristics of a man's identity (Gori, 1999). Throughout *Investigation of a Citizen above Suspicion*, Petri makes a link between corrupt patriarchal fascistic power and fear of sexual impotence, as the inspector's wounded masculinity seems very much like another motivation for his crime. In a scene of almost ludicrous machismo, the inspector tells his superior that he was having an affair with the murder victim, to which the sleazy commissioner (Gianni Santuccio) responds, unphased by this incriminating revelation, 'How was it? Good?' Later, when the inspector confesses to his crime and insists that his motive was Terzi's mockery of his impotence, the commissioner and his men are still not stirred, as though exposing this fact would uncover not only the corruption within the institution but also the inadequacies of the men who uphold it.

The work of Elio Petri presents a different approach to political cinema, one that puts individual subjectivity and psychology at the forefront of political critique, much to the frustration of some of his leftist peers. In response to the argument that his style is too caricatural, he argues: 'Unfortunately, reality is caricature. I believe that cinema should stress this, even if it means resorting to very popular forms' (in Georgakas and Rubenstein, 1985: 58). This sentiment is applicable to many of the films mentioned in this dossier, which demonstrate the effectiveness of using a popular, accessible genre to communicate political statements and debates to a large audience. For Petri, no matter what genre he is working within, his work is simply a reflection of an absurdly convoluted political reality and the horrors of modern life. With *Investigation of a Citizen above Suspicion*, he successfully utilises and subverts the thriller to question the conduct and function of the police, and the film would come to define the director's enduring legacy and continues to find resonance today.

References

Georgakas, D. and Rubenstein, L. (1985). *The Cineaste Interviews: On the Art and Politics of the Cinema*. London: Pluto Press.

Gili, J. A. (2013). *Writings on Cinema and Life: Elio Petri*. New York: Contra Mundum Press.

Gori, G. (1999). 'Model of Masculinity: Mussolini, The "New Italian of the Fascist Era"'. *International Journal of the History of Sport*, 16(4), 27–61.

Portis, L. (2010). 'The Director Who Must (Not?) Be Forgotten: Elio Petri and the Legacy of Italian Political Cinema Part 2'. *Film International*, 46(8), 42–50.

Resmini, M. (2018). 'The Worker as Figure: On Elio Petri's *The Working Class Goes to Heaven*'. *Diacritics*, 46(4), 72–95.

Williams, E. C. (2013). '*Investigation of a Citizen above Suspicion*: The Long Harm of the Law'. *Criterion*. Retrieved from: www.criterion.com/current/posts/2979-investigation-of-a-citizen-above-suspicion-the-long-harm-of-the-law

9

Killer Cop (*La polizia ha le mani legate*), Luciano Ercoli, 1975

MaoHui Deng

Figure 10 *Killer Cop* (1975), courtesy of Raro Video

Killer Cop, or more accurately translated from the Italian title *La polizia ha le mani legate*, *The Police Have their Hands Tied*, is directed by Luciano Ercoli and was released in Italy in March 1975. The film features many actors from the Italian film industry who worked in both commercial filmmaking and auteur cinema, like Claudio Cassinelli, Franco Fabrizi, Bruno Zanin and Valeria D'Obici (who made her debut in the film). It also stars the American actor Arthur Kennedy. The film's narrative is thrust into action when a bomb goes off in the lobby of a busy hotel in Milan: the protagonist, Matteo Rolandi (Cassinelli), a commissioner, is one of the witnesses and sets out to find the perpetrators, and an honest magistrate, Armando Di Federico (Kennedy), conducts the official investigation but is met with bureaucratic roadblock and corruption. At every step, however, a shadowy organisation that has its tentacles in the police and government attempts to get rid of the evidence before Rolandi and Di Federico can uncover them.

This act of terror, which happens early in the film, was inspired by the Piazza Fontana bombing in 1969, when a bomb exploded at the National Agricultural Bank in Milan, killing seventeen people and injuring many more, and it is important to situate *Killer Cop* in the socio-political context of Italy in the late 1960s and the 1970s in order to understand how the lived experiences of Italians at that time might have bled into the film's narrative and aesthetics. Backdropped against the student protests in 1968 and the large-scale strikes from factory workers demanding better pay conditions in the *autunno caldo* (hot autumn) of 1969, the Piazza Fontana incident was initially attributed to and blamed on left-wing anarchists. Many left-wing activists were rounded up by the state and one of them, the anarchist railroad worker Giuseppe Pinelli, subsequently fell to his death from a fourth-floor window at Milan's central police station. This incident caused nationwide outrage and has haunted Italy ever since. At first, the police attributed his death to suicide whilst many members of the public, particularly those on the left, insisted the police had murdered Pinelli. Finally, in 1975, a compromise between these two versions was provided, and in the 1975 report, the explanation offered was 'The air in the room was heavy, oppressive. The window was opened [and as Pinelli] went over to the balcony for a breath of fresh air, he felt dizzy, he put out his hands in the wrong direction, his body fell over the railings' (in Foot, 2009: 184). The official excuse – that Pinelli fell from the window because he was suffering from a severe illness – has subsequently been widely ridiculed and, after several years of investigation since the publication of the report, it became clear that the Piazza Fontana bombing was conducted by the far right, although a specific group has never publicly claimed responsibility.

During the 1970s, a series of other bomb attacks and terror incidents occurred throughout Italy that were designed to create a sense of suspicion towards the left in the public consciousness. These acts of terror, known as *stragismo* (derived from the word *strage*, or massacre), contributed more generally towards what has come to be described as the 'strategy of tension' adopted by extreme-right groups 'whose aim was to create an atmosphere of subversion and fear in the country so as to promote a turn to an authoritarian type of government' (Cento Bull, 2012: 19). Coupled with portions of the government and the police actively contributing to the tension through their seemingly being unaccountable to anyone, as evidenced by incidents such as that involving Pinelli, there was not only a deep atmosphere of distrust towards almost everyone but a more prevalent sense of all-encompassing conspiracy engendered by the strategy of tension.

Killer Cop not only takes the bomb attack at the Piazza Fontana building as inspiration but goes one step further by including television footage from the actual funerals of the Piazza Fontana victims, and in doing so, blurs the line between on-screen fiction and off-screen fact. With the Piazza Fontana incident as a landmark moment in 1969 for both the politics and the cultural imagination of the nation, and with the strategy of tension as a backdrop, a decade of tense political unrest began in Italy. The right, including and supported by portions of the state machine and the Italian secret service, continued with their efforts to create instability. On the other hand, the left carried out their own armed struggle, in large parts as a response to the violent activities of the right. These multiple intimidations and assassinations were carried out by *both* the political right and left, and they worked to further create an environment of fear and mistrust in Italy. Marking the end of one of the most violent decades since World War II, this series of events culminated in the kidnapping and murder of the former Prime Minister Aldo Moro by the far-left paramilitary group *Brigate Rosse* (Red Brigades) in 1978, and the bombing of the Bologna Central railway station in 1980 that killed eighty-five people and was attributed to members of the far-right *Nuclei Armati Rivoluzionari* (Armed Revolutionary Nuclei).

As a result of these violent, politically motivated actions, the 1970s in Italy is commonly referred to as the *anni di piombo*, or the 'years of lead'. The phrase used to describe the decade is derived from the 1981 German film *Die bleierne Zeit* (*Marianna and Juliane*) directed by Margarethe von Trotta. The film did exceptionally well at the Venice Film Festival and the Italian title, *Anni di piombo*, which is a literal translation of the German title, started entering into popular discourse when referring to the 1970s. In large parts, the phrase 'anni di piombo' is meant to refer to the leaden weight of the events that happened in the decade. Beyond that, though, Alan O'Leary notes, the phrase unfortunately also connotes an imagery of bullets exchanged and in turn 'implicitly excludes the bombings characteristic of right-wing terrorism' (2011: 8). This connotation is compounded by the impression that, during the *anni di piombo*, cinema, and most cultural and public discourses, predominantly focused on the atrocities of the left, and this imbalance has significant consequences in Italy's public memory. As Tom Behan suggests, most young people in Italy in the new millennium think of the *anni di piombo* as the 'years of left-wing terrorism', forgetting a lot of the atrocities were carried out by the right, consequently resulting in 'enormous historical distortion' (2006: 168).

According to Ruth Glynn, Giancarlo Lombardi and O'Leary, there are a few reasons as to why there seems to be more films about left-wing terrorism made during the decade. Firstly, acts of terror from the left represent a particular point of interest to left-wing filmmakers who 'Have taken upon themselves the responsibility of articulating the meaning of terrorist violence practised by members of their own constituency', whereas political violence does not represent so much a problem to be examined in detail but an ideal to be attained for the far right (2012: 18). Secondly, left-wing terror lent itself well to the screen because the perpetrators of the violence were very adept at using audio-visual images to capture the attention of the public and draw attention to themselves (2012: 18–19). On the other hand, because of the widespread anonymity and invisibility of the right-wing terrorists, films that sought to depict the strategy of tension on screen frequently resorted to the conspiracy mode of address. For Glynn, Lombardi and O'Leary, this approach towards filmmaking could in turn paradoxically further confirm a world view pushed by the far right, which is a world that is run by violence and should be ultimately run by an authoritarian government (2012: 19).

Killer Cop is one of the films from this period that attempted to articulate the conspiratorial tensions underlying contemporary Italian society, sitting neatly in the *poliziottesco filone* that proliferated and was made cheaply in the 1970s. In Italy, *filone* refers to a cycle of films that is produced very quickly in order to capitalise on a particular film's success. In a sense, the concept of *filone* is similar to that of the genre but is more temporally specific as the demands of the audience shift very quickly – when a *filone* falls out of fashion, a new one replaces it. According to O'Leary, the *poliziottesco*, or the cop film, contains a few recurring features: a commissioner protagonist who is restrained by a media or magistrate that is too concerned with procedures and civil rights; right-wing shady figures with a lot of political power who aim to have the commissioner, and anyone who gets in their way, eliminated; a woman love interest who is either a side character or a threat to the hero; conventional action sequences that are also very violent and regularly feature the death of an innocent passer-by caught in the situation; and didactic dialogue that details the ideology and aims of the shadowy figure's desire to take over the state (2011: 93–94).

Narratively, the characters in *Killer Cop* follow all the *poliziottesco* features as outlined by O'Leary. The protagonist, Rolandi, is a commissioner who is characterised as an avid reader of *Moby Dick*, very unsubtly paralleling his quest for truth to Ahab's obsessive expedition to capture the white whale in the novel. Despite this, the villains are always one step ahead of him, which prevents him from solving the crime. Likewise, Magistrate Di Federico is unflinchingly upright in his official investigation, but his pursuit is also stopped by the all-encompassing corrupt forces in the police and government. Papaya (Sara Sperati), the woman who frequently has sex with Rolandi, functions as a sexualised spectacle for the audience's gaze, as the camera focuses on her body both in and out of underwear. In addition, she is also revealed to be a threat to Rolandi as she is controlled by a higher unknown and nefarious force, regularly conspiring to put him in harm's way.

Throughout the film, there is a general sense of distrust saturating society. Right after the bombing, for instance, the film cuts to a sequence on a tram where the passengers, reading the day's newspapers, quarrel with one another over who to blame, pointing their fingers at both the fascists and the communists, at both the right and the left. Beyond that, the individual perpetrators of the crimes and acts of terror are regularly shown to be controlled by bigger unknown figures, and these shadowy people that permeate all walks of life are largely anonymous, although they are predominantly coded to be of wealth and status. When these characters are on screen, they are often in a large room drinking alcohol and smoking cigars, and their faces are masked by wide-angle shots, distorted by glass refractions and, at times, completely shrouded in darkness. In turn, a deep sense of conspiracy, where everyone could be contributing to the atmosphere of terror, is fuelled.

Compared with the high-brow political films made by auteur figures like Francesco Rosi and Elio Petri, film critics of the time used the phrase *poliziottescho* to pejoratively describe this cycle of films about the strategy of tension (Bondanella, 2009: 453). The *poliziotteschi* were understood as cheap and low-brow films that capitalised on the nation's politics as a 'trendy' backdrop for financial gains, and this economical and commercial mode of production is evident in *Killer Cop*. Not only are there throwaway sex scenes in the film which are included mainly for spectacle but the era's material culture is also indexed, as Rolandi's Mercedes-Benz 300 SE Coupé is constantly acknowledged by the other characters who are all decked in the latest fashion. Visually, the film is littered with shots of people looking into and spying through mirrors – which reduces the need to film a reverse shot (thus saving money) – and these shots work to further the film's central conspiratorial theme and atmosphere. Aurally, the score composed by Stelvio Cipriani extensively references the earlier film scores of *La polizia ringrazia* (*Execution Squad*, Steno, 1972) and *La polizia sta a guadare* (*The Great Kidnapping*, Roberto Infascelli, 1973) that he also composed – Cipriani is known for recycling the music that he composed for his '*La polizia*' films, using the same theme through different arrangements.

In turn, the visual and aural elements of *Killer Cop* become a way to archive and surface Italy's political traumas into the wider film cycle, echoing Austin Fisher's suggestion that the *poliziottescho filone* operates 'as a ritual recognition of always-already accepted political tenets' (2014: 176) and that these films 'are repositories of cultural memory and sites of popular trauma' which articulated the tension felt during the *anni di piombo* (2017: 263). This is to say, these films are not political with a capital 'P', as films by Rosi and Petri might be read as, and they do not necessarily offer a nuanced diagnosis of Italy's political situation. Rather, for Fisher, *poliziottescho* films like *Killer Cop* enact a ritualistic articulation and acknowledgement of the situation, taking 'corruption and conspiracy as an accepted starting point and therefore offer little pretence towards complex analysis or investigation into its precise political motivations on behalf of their viewers' (2014: 177). In fact, *Killer Cop* never unmasks the people or forces who are ultimately responsible for the atrocities committed at the start of the film, and the film ends with a final shot of him tailing a member of the government. Before it ends, captions enter the film announcing that Rolandi was the first to arrive at the scene to find a prosecutor, who was shot and left in a ditch, dead. Italy's political context, then, becomes an aid to 'the broader construction of a believable backdrop for the film's plot' and, in some sense, is a MacGuffin for filmmakers to capitalise on narratives of suspense and thrill (Fisher, 2019: 62).

However, this is not to say that the film, and the wider *filone*, is not political. For Mary P. Wood, 'conspiracy theories and attempts to visualize and put a face to those responsible for atrocities represent a failure in the hegemonic process because they signal the inability of a power elite to impose its own views of events' (2012: 32). Put differently, films that told stories about the terror inflicted by the far-right groups through the strategy of tension, in being unable to pin the crime to a certain person or a particular group of people, draw the audience's attention to – and potentially also critique – the ways in which power in Italian society is unevenly distributed. Even though, by the end of the film, the audience is still unclear as to who the perpetrators are and even though the death toll is rising, *Killer Cop* makes it abundantly clear that the world order, one that a largely invisible and rich group of people try to impose, has not succeeded. Seen from this viewpoint, *Killer Cop*, as a *poliziottesco*, is not just a film with a lot of fast-paced and thrilling action sequences that are injected with a good dose of conspiracy. On top of the excitement engendered by the film's narrative and aesthetics, *Killer Cop* provides the audience a way in to recognise and think through the socio-politics of everyday people living in Italy in the *anni di piombo*.

References

Behan, T. (2006). 'Allende, Berlinguer, Pinochet ... and Dario Fo'. In A. Cento Bull and A. Giorgio (Eds), *Speaking Out and Silencing: Culture, Society and Politics in Italy in the 1970s*. Oxford: Legenda, 161–171.

Bondanella, P. (2009). *A History of Italian Cinema*. New York: Continuum.
Cento Bull, A. (2012). *Italian Neofascism: The Strategy of Tension and the Politics of Nonreconciliation*. Oxford: Berghahn Books.
Ferraresi, F. (1996). *Threats to Democracy: The Radical Right in Italy after the War*. Princeton, NJ: Princeton University Press.
Fisher, A. (2014). '*Il braccio violento della legge*: Revelation, Conspiracy and the Politics of Violence in the Poliziottesco'. *Journal of Italian Cinema and Media Studies* 2(2), 167–181.
Fisher, A. (2017). 'Italian Popular Film Genres'. In F. Burke (Ed.), *A Companion to Popular Italian Cinema*. Chichester, West Sussex: John Wiley and Sons, 250–266.
Fisher, A. (2019). *Blood in the Streets: Histories of Violence in Italian Crime Cinema*. Edinburgh: Edinburgh University Press.
Foot, J. (2009). *Italy's Divided Memory*. Basingstoke: Palgrave Macmillan.
Glynn, R., Lombardi, G. and O'Leary, A. (2012). 'Introduction: Terrorism, Italian Style'. In R. Glynn, G. Lombardi and A. O'Leary (Eds), *Terrorism, Italian Style: Representations of Political Violence in Contemporary Italian Cinema*. London: IGRS Books, 13–25.
O'Leary, A. (2011). *Tragedia all'italiana: Italian Cinema and Italian Terrorisms, 1970–2010*. Bern, Switzerland: Peter Lang.
Wood, M. P. (2012). 'Navigating the Labyrinth: Cinematic Investigations of Right-Wing Terrorism'. In R. Glynn, G. Lombardi and A. O'Leary (Eds), *Terrorism, Italian Style: Representations of Political Violence in Contemporary Italian Cinema*. London: IGRS Books, 29–44.

10

West Germany: Terrorism on the doorstep

Andy Willis

Figure 11 *Knife in the Head* (1978), courtesy of StudioCanal Germany

Whilst the Federal Republic of Germany (*Bundesrepublik Deutschland*), commonly referred to as West Germany, was the site of some of the most notorious acts of politically motivated terrorism of the 1970s, the political thriller was much less prevalent within its cinematic output than one might expect. This is particularly the case when one compares it to the industries of France or Italy. One of the reasons for this was the changes the West German film industry underwent in the late 1960s and 1970s. Unlike France and Italy, the commercial side of the industry contracted during this period, seeing commercial filmmaking becoming much less prominent than it had been in earlier eras. Tim Bergfelder argues that this represented a change in the industry's agenda 'towards an aesthetically and politically different form of cinema' driven by the emergence of the New German Cinema filmmakers of the 1960s and 1970s. He continues:

> At the heart of this agenda was the desire to replace a cinema of producers and distributors ... with a cinema of *auteurs*. These were understood to be self-determined creative artists whose work moreover fulfilled a significant social function, by intervening in political issues ranging from the Vietnam War, the unresolved legacy of Germany's Nazi past, and later in the 1970s the rise of urban terrorism.
>
> 2005: 236

This group of *auteurs* is usually identified as having at its core Alexander Kluge, Rainer Werner Fassbinder, Werner Herzog, Volker Schlöndorff, Margarethe von Trotta and Wim Wenders.

Although levels of production of commercial cinema in West Germany were not as high as in key international production bases such as Italy, West Germany was used as a setting for a number of Cold War thrillers. These saw international filmmakers making work that can broadly be labelled as political thrillers due to their stories of spies and intrigue against a backdrop of the Cold War. *The Man Between* (Carol Reed, 1953) is an early example of the use of Berlin as a setting for such stories, with its tale of a woman visiting the city and becoming drawn into the political intrigue that is shown as being part of everyday life there. From the mid-1960s, a number of German-set adaptations of thriller novels used the machinations of the Cold War setting as key to their plots. These included films based on John le Carré novels such as *The Spy Who Came in from the Cold* (Martin Ritt, 1965) and *The Looking Glass War* (Frank Pierson, 1970) and others based on books by Len Deighton (*Funeral in Berlin*, Guy Hamilton, 1966) and Adam Hall (*The Berlin Memorandum*, retitled *The Quiller Memorandum*, Michael Anderson, 1966). These continued into the 1970s, with *The Odessa File* (Ronald Neame, 1974) adapted from a work by Frederick Forsyth, author of *The Day of the Jackal* (1971), which was itself made into a successful film released in 1973, one of the most interesting examples.

In West Germany in the 1970s, the intrigues of the political thriller could be found more commonly on television than in features made by domestic film production companies. West German television companies had had some significant input into the early work of a number of New German Cinema figures, in particular, Fassbinder. In doing so, they sought to make programmes that would reflect the contemporary issues facing West German society. One of the major series, which launched in 1970, was the police procedural *Tatort* (*Crime Scene*, 1970 onwards). The year that it was first broadcast also saw the formation of the Red Army Faction (RAF, *Rote Armee Fraktion*), or the Baader-Meinhof Group. Following this, the 1970s would see a range of actions such as bank robberies, bombing and assassinations that ushered in a period of great social unrest and social anxiety. The tension that existed across West German society in the 1970s would be addressed by a number of thriller-related feature films made in the decade such as *The Lost Honour of Katharina Blum* (*Die Verlorene Ehre der Katharina Blum*, 1975) and *Knife in the Head* (*Messer im Kopf*, Reinhard Hauff, 1978). It was against this backdrop that *Tatort* found a significant audience, and Bärbel Göbel-Stolz suggests that this unease helped the television companies, when she argues that 'The ongoing political unrest ... may have ensured that funding through government channels was easily received for a tale dealing with crime, morality and ethics' (2016: 193).

Given this context, it is perhaps less surprising than one might at first think to find that one of the outliers of the European political thriller of the 1970s had its origin in West German television. *Dead Pigeon on Beethoven Street* (*Tote Taube in der Beethovenstraße*, 1972) was directed by American Samuel Fuller, a filmmaker renowned for his tough thrillers of the 1950s and 1960s, for the West German television series *Tatort*. The series was produced by West Germany's regional production companies, who each contributed episodes to a season with a different investigator working in each city or region, with creatives being given a clear blueprint. As Göbel-Stolz states, 'When Tatort was created, many rules were established to ensure that the series could have a recognizable brand image, despite the numerous producers, actors, writers, and directors involved in the different regions' (2016: 196). The fact that within this structure each regional broadcaster was given a level of independence to make their own version of *Tatort* led to the head of TV drama at WDR (*Westdeutscher Rundfunk*), Günter Rohrbach, hiring Fuller to contribute an episode set in Cologne. Fuller was paired with producer Joachim von Mengershausen, who was a significant figure in the nurturing of young European filmmakers such as Wim Wenders. Fuller approached the commission as a piece of cinema rather than television, something reflected in the fact that his episode was shot on 35mm and boasted Polish cinematographer Jerzy Lipman, who had worked as a director of photography with directors Andrzej Wajda and Roman Polanski. According to Fuller, the plot of *Dead Pigeon on Beethoven Street* was inspired by the Profumo affair, which had seen the downfall of politician John Profumo, the Secretary of State for War in the British government, following an affair with a nineteen-year-old model and showgirl. He stated that the 'scandal was big news in those days, filling the papers with real-life tales of blackmailed politicians and high-class call girls. In *Dead Pigeon*, an international syndicate is blackmailing diplomats' (2002: 450–451).

Whilst the story suggests potential for a political thriller along the lines of those developing across Europe in the early 1970s, ultimately, Fuller's film, which was released theatrically outside West Germany, stretches the credibility of the thriller into the realm of comedy, creating something more akin to a deconstruction of the form. So, whilst *Tatort* was known for its more realistic portraits of contemporary West Germany, Fuller was instead making a self-conscious 'yarn ... a tongue-in-cheek adventure' (2002: 450) that was full of 'high jinks and hilarity' (2002: 452). This is reflected in the opening of the film, which sees some members of the cast and crew, including Fuller himself, dressed in costumes and hats for Cologne's famous carnival intercut with images of festivities on the street. In a burst of self-reflexivity, members of the editing, sound, camera and script teams are seemingly in despair at the material they have to work with. As this opening suggests, of all the films that may be encompassed by the term political thriller, *Dead Pigeon on Beethoven Street* is certainly one of the strangest.

Another director who emerged from television, where he worked on *Tatort*, was Wolfgang Petersen. As well as directing episodes of that police procedural, he was also involved in high-profile work such as *Van der Valk und die Reichen* (*Van der Valk and the Rich*, 1973), an adaptation of the crime novel by Nicolas Freeling with Frank Finlay in the lead role. This indicates that Peterson was interested in exploring popular forms, including the thriller.

However, some examples, such as his first theatrical release *One or the Other* (*Einer von uns beiden*, 1974), touch on areas that could have been developed more politically, even if allegorically, in this case, blackmail and corruption in the context of university academic life. Peterson would develop his career, which ultimately led to Hollywood blockbusters, with two collaborators he first worked with on episodes of *Tatort*, producer Günter Rohrbach and actor Jürgen Prochnow. As the 1970s ended, they would work together on one of the most successful West German films of all time, *Das Boot* (*The Boat*, 1981).

Whilst Wolfgang Peterson is an example of a director who avoided directly political material, the urgency of the political situation in West Germany in the 1970s, fuelled by acts of political violence by those acting on behalf of groups opposed to the state and by the state itself, led to a number of other filmmakers making work that explicitly engaged with it. As Julian Preece notes, 'Film and political violence went hand in hand in the late 1970s and early 1980s', going on to argue that 'The links between cinema, in particular the West German New Wave or New German Cinema Movement, and the RAF and its related groupings are manifold' (2008: 213). Volker Schlöndorff was one of those whose work directly addressed the political situation of the day either directly or through allegories. The latter can be seen in films such as the historical drama *Michael Kohlhass – Der Rebell*, which boasts playwright Edward Bond amongst its writers, that considered social class and injustice. As Jason Wood explores in the next chapter of this dossier, in 1975, Schlöndorff collaborated with Margarethe von Trotta on an adaptation of Heinrich Böll's book *The Lost Honour of Katharina Blum*, a film that can certainly be considered a complex example of the European political thriller. This complexity is set up by an opening which, like *Dead Pigeon on Beethoven Street*, utilises the setting of Cologne's carnival, a site where identity is unfixed and masquerade is always near. As Lawrence Webb argues, the film reveals an 'ability to reconcile such urgent, contemporary themes with narrative drive and stylistic patterns of the Hollywood thriller' (2014: 296). He goes on to report that Schlöndorff himself intended the film as an intervention in the politics of the day, and he quotes the director, saying that 'Katharina Blum was produced in the middle of the action, in the heat of the moment. We were using film as a weapon. It was very polemical, part of a larger political struggle, and one didn't quite know where the film stopped and real life began' (2014: 297). Margarethe von Trotta would further use the form of the thriller, at least in part, to explore the motivations behind acts of violent terrorism with *The Second Awakening of Christa Klages* (*Das zweite Erwachen der Christa Klages*, 1978), which follows the titular character as she is driven to rob banks and then go on the run. *Time Out* observed at the time that von Trotta was 'one of the few film-makers to portray terrorists convincingly' (Dickinson, 2003: 1064). In 1979, Rainer Werner Fassbinder would also release a film that focused on a group of terrorists plotting to kidnap an industrialist, *The Third Generation* (*Die Dritte Generation*). A rather idiosyncratic, darkly comedic exploration of the dynamics of the group, this approach to such a raw contemporary subject did attract some criticism.

Another film that directly addresses the impact of extreme politics on West German society is *Knife in the Head* (*Messer im Kopf*, 1978). Director Reinhard Hauff and writer Peter Schneider create a film that utilises the format of the thriller to suggest a society where both sides of the political spectrum are manipulative and ultimately must be questioned. Writing in *Senses of Cinema*, Robert M. Stowe argues that this marks *Knife in the Head* out from many of the other films collected under the label New German Cinema, saying that '*Knife in the Head* differs from these other films in its linear narrative structure and fairly conventional, 1970's Hollywood style story-telling along the lines of the paranoia thriller modelled around a central character with whom the audience can identify' (2011). The film explores this through the piecing together of the central character's memories of a night he cannot remember but during which the police use force to break up a left-leaning social centre. As he lies in hospital, he becomes a site of struggle between those on the left and the police representing the state, with each hoping to project on to him their version of the evening's events. As Preece notes, this reflects something of a middle-of-the-road position that is offered by the film, and one he suggests was also held by the director. He argues that 'The end of his *Messer im Kopf* (1978), showing a police gunman and his recuperated victim tormenting each other, is part of a cycle which, it seems, will never end … Hauff sees both sides behaving badly' (2008: 216). This is quite different from something like *The Lost Honour of Katherina Blum* which ultimately shows its lead character, Blum, as a victim of state oppression that forces her into an act of violence, something that can then be exploited by the powers that be. As Webb puts it:

> If terrorism remains resolutely offscreen, it operates as a structuring absence on proceedings. Though it is suggested at the end that Ludwig may not have been a terrorist after all, his guilt or innocence is ultimately of no real consequence to the plot. The political thrust of the film is rather to forward the notion that repressive measures produce violence as a structural effect.
>
> 2014: 296

Hauff would continue to explore the issue of terrorism in *Stammheim: The Baader-Meinhof Gang on Trial* (*Stammheim: Die Baader-Meinhof-Gruppe vor Gericht*, 1986), a film that won the Golden Bear at the Berlin Film Festival. Here, scriptwriter Stefan Aust, who wrote many things about the Red Army Faction in various media, uses transcripts from the trial to create an air of truthfulness to the project.

The twenty-first century has seen a number of films produced in the now reunited Germany that explore the political past in the form of the thriller. These have included a number of works that have revisited the turbulent decade of the 1970s and the terrorist groups such as the RAF that are now seen to embody the politics of the era, or the legacy of their actions. The most obvious is *The Baader Meinhof Complex* (*Der Baader Meinhof Komplex*, 2008), which tells the story of the RAF and was directed by Uli Edel, another filmmaker who had emerged from television in the late 1970s. The aftermath of terrorism on individuals is explored by Volker Schlöndorff in *The Legend of Rita* (*Die Stille nach dem Schuß*, 2000) and by Christian Petzold in *The State I Am in* (*Die innere Sicherheit*, 2000). Petzold would circle around the form of the political thriller in 2012 with *Barbara*. In that instance, he certainly used moments of jeopardy and tension, particularly around Barbara's relationship, if not fully embracing the thriller format. As Declan Clarke notes in a later chapter of this dossier, in its dealing with a doctor's ultimately flawed desire to leave the German Democratic Republic (GDR) for the west, *Barbara* echoes the East German film *Die Flucht* (*The Flight*, 1977).

One of the most successful of the twenty-first-century films that used the form of the thriller is *The Lives of Others* (*Das Leben der Anderen*, 2006), which won widespread acclaim, including the Oscar for Best Foreign Language Film in 2007. The film tells the story of an East German Stasi officer, who whilst monitoring a liberal writer begins to question his previously unquestioning commitment to the government of the GDR. Director Florian Henckel von Donnersmarck constructs a *mise en scène* for the film that helps recreate the surveillance regime of 1980s East Germany, utilising shadows and an array of dark green and blue hues. Paul Cooke links the film to a number of thrillers, some of which I would consider political thrillers, that are concerned with issues of surveillance, when he observes: '*Das Leben der Anderen* is part of a long tradition of films, from Alfred Hitchcock's *Rear Window* (1954) to Tony Scott's *Enemy of the State* (1998), which explore the question of surveillance' (2012: 115), before going on to compare it to another American film, which can also be considered a political thriller, *The Conversation* (1974). Cooke also notes that *The Lives of Others* has garnered criticism for using mainstream, commercial film form to address a political subject. For example, he highlights Barry Langford, whom he says argues this is an example of 'where emotion is prioritised over critical distance' (2012: 114). This echoes the criticism that was aimed at the films of Costa-Gavras and others who embraced the political thriller in the early 1970s, and shows that the debates around film form and political content are still relevant today.

References

Bergfelder, T. (2005). *International Adventures: German Popular Cinema and European Co-Productions in the 1960s*. Oxford: Berghahn Books.
Cooke, P. (2012). *Contemporary German Cinema*. Manchester: Manchester University Press.
Dickinson, F. (2003). 'The Second Awakening of Christa Klages'. In J. Pym (Ed.), *Time Out Film Guide* (11th ed.). London: Penguin, 1064.
Fuller, S. (2002). *A Third Face: My Tale of Writing, Fighting, and Filmmaking*. New York: Alfred A. Knopf.
Göbel-Stolz, B. (2016). 'Once Upon a Crime: Tatort, Germany's Longest Running Police Procedural'. In L. Powell and R. Shandley (Eds), *German Television: Historical and Theoretical Perspectives*. Oxford: Berghahn Books, 193–214.

Preece, J. (2008). 'Reinscribing the German Autumn: Heinrich Breloer's Todesspiel and the Two Clusters of German "Terrorist" Films'. *German Monitor*, 70, 213–229.

Stowe, R. M. (2011). '*Knife in the Head*: German Social Realism Meets Cinema Verité'. *Senses of Cinema*, 60. Retrieved from: www.sensesofcinema.com/2011/feature-articles/knife-in-the-head-german-social-realism-meets-cinema-verite/

Webb, L. (2014). *The Cinema of Urban Crisis: Seventies Film and the Reinvention of the City*. Amsterdam: Amsterdam University Press.

11

Neither intentional nor accidental, but unavoidable: *The Lost Honour of Katharina Blum*

Jason Wood

Figure 12 *The Lost Honour of Katharina Blum* (1975), courtesy of StudioCanal

Adapted from the 1974 novel of the same name by Cologne-born author Heinrich Böll, whose major works include *Billiards at Half past Nine* (*Billard um halb zehn*, 1959), *The Clown* (*Ansichten eines Clowns*, 1963) and *The Safety Net* (*Fürsorgliche Belagerung*, 1979) and who won the Nobel Prize for Literature in 1972, *The Lost Honour of Katharina Blum* (*Die verlorene Ehre der Katharina Blum*, 1975), subtitled by Böll *How Violence Can Arise and What It Can Lead to*, captures the pervading climate of fear and paranoia that gripped 1970s Germany. Böll focuses on the power of the state and the lack of autonomy of the individual in the face of this power. The novel was remarkably prescient in its consideration of the manipulation of facts by the media and how the media effectively colluded with the state to breed suspicion, paranoia and distrust.

Today, in an era in which press intrusion, the twisting and manipulation of truth and media shaming have extended beyond print and television into an entirely new and ungovernable worldwide digital domain, the film, and Böll's source material, feel as relevant if not more so today than on its original release in 1975. The hugely influential writer and film historian Thomas Elsaesser asserted that '*The Lost Honour of Katharina Blum* is not an illuminating film about the German press' (1989: 62). He also commented that one learns little about the political establishment from it and frequently solely credits the film's direction to Volker Schlöndorff, but this was in 1989. One feels that in the current environment and with the ghastly public appetite for judgement and condemnation by media trial, Elsaesser's opinion may have been markedly different today. As Amy Taubin points out, 'few political films transcend their historic moment. Yet watching Volker Schlöndorff and Margarethe von Trotta's *The Lost Honour of Katharina Blum* today is an uncanny experience' (2003).

Published in 1974, Böll's novel is set at the height of social and political unrest in West Germany during the often violent activities of the Baader-Meinhof gang. In one incident, a bank was robbed and a security guard murdered. The next day, though lacking significant evidence, the nation's largest newspaper, the *Bild-Zeitung*, attributed the crime to the gang. Böll, a contemporary of writers including Günter Grass and Martin Walser, who offered astute commentaries on post-war Germany, condemned this trial by headline in an article for *Der Spiegel*, a centre-left publication known for its rigorous investigative journalism and uncovering of political scandals, and rapidly became the target of hate mail, anonymous calls and indignant editorials. Böll subsequently transformed his own experience of media intrusion, public shaming and accusations of terrorist sympathies into a novel in which the central protagonist is Katharina Blum, a young female housekeeper in the employ of a wealthy family. After spending the night with a young man she meets on an evening out, Blum finds herself questioned by the police when it transpires that her lover is a young radical on the run for suspected terrorist activities. As the media picks up on the story, Blum's history with the man is exaggerated to more than a one-night affair, and she quickly finds her life systematically undone by the distortions of a corrupt press concerned only with presenting the most salacious story. Böll's novel was a critical and commercial success, though the same publications that slandered the author downplayed its chiming with the public by deciding not to print the bestseller lists Böll topped in their pages.

As a film, *The Lost Honour of Katharina Blum* marked the sole directorial collaboration between two key figures in New German Cinema, Volker Schlöndorff and Margarethe von Trotta. Co-directing and co-adapting, the then husband and wife team, who had apparently decided to adapt Böll's novel before it was published after discussing its contents with the author, cast Angela Winkler in the title role as the proud but relatively impoverished maid for a prosperous attorney whose fateful night with young radical Ludwig (Jürgen Prochnow) leads her to the attentions of a salacious journalist, Werner Tötges (the recently deceased Dieter Laser, who would go on to find fame as Dr Heiter in Tom Six's *The Human Centipede*, 2009), under pressure to double down on radicals, and the vengeful, broadly misogynistic police inspector Kommissar Beizmenne (Mario Adorf) looking to make an arrest.

Dragged reluctantly into the spotlight, Blum, nicknamed by the press as 'the nun' for her hitherto unimpeachable morality, finds herself a police subject and the victim of a vicious media smear in which she is portrayed as a whore after circumstantial evidence suggests that she had for some time been Ludwig's mistress. Her limits of dignity and sanity are pushed to their threshold as her apartment is ransacked and she is ritually humiliated, initially by being subjected to a public strip search by her male and female inquisitors. Consequently, Blum's personal life is defiled. Refusing to buckle, and remaining resolute and dignified throughout her degrading ordeal, Blum is nonetheless vilified and very publicly, physically and verbally insulted by some members of her community. She is forced to bear witness to the extreme toll her ordeal places on her elderly and dying mother, who is herself stalked by Tötges in her hospital room as he seeks to extract from her a deathbed statement about her daughter's actions.

Initially, viewing the activities of the police and the authorities as perhaps a necessary evil and part of the machinations of the wider system, the actions of Tötges, a philandering narcissist with unscrupulous morals, prove too much for Blum, who, finally cognisant of the collusion between the police and the far-right press in terms of suppressing and ultimately punishing those with the temerity to question the counter-terrorism policies of the government, exacts her own violent revenge, shooting him dead after he attempts to cajole her into allowing him to write her side of the story after first aggressively attempting to seduce her. In the film's epilogue, Tötges, for whom 'the duty of the press is to inform', is given a sombre televised state funeral in which the owner of the newspaper extols his virtues whilst asserting 'the shots were aimed at the freedom of the press, one of the most precious values of our young democracy. Freedom of the press is the core of everything: well-being, democracy, pluralism, diversity of opinion. Whoever attacks the paper attacks us all.' Schlöndorff and von Trotta respond with some biting closing words of their own, appearing as a final title: 'Descriptions of journalistic practices are neither intentional nor accidental, but unavoidable.'

In France during the early 1960s, Volker Schlöndorff got his first opportunities in filmmaking working as an assistant director with acclaimed directors such as Alain Resnais, Jean-Pierre Melville and Louis Malle. During this period, he grew increasingly interested in the way in which political ideas could be expressed through films. In this regard, discussing his 1966 debut *Young Törless* (*Der junge Törless*), based on Robert Musil's novel, the Criterion website states that it:

> was not only the first of his many literary adaptations, it was also something of a New German Cinema call to arms, a political allegory about Germany's social history set in a boys' boarding school

at the turn of the twentieth century. More stinging commentaries on the state of Germany-then-and-now followed in the seventies: *The Lost Honor of Katharina Blum* (codirected with Margarethe von Trotta, Schlöndorff's wife at the time), *Coup de grâce*, and his grandest success, the Oscar- and Palme d'or-winning *The Tin Drum*, a brilliant adaptation of Günter Grass's metaphorical novel about the horrors of World War II.

www.criterion.com/films/926-young-trless

Described by the Independent Cinema Office, quoting *Sight and Sound*, as 'the indefatigable feminist of the once-New German Cinema' (Independent Cinema Office, 2019), Margarethe von Trotta made her directorial debut with *The Lost Honour of Katharina Blum*. As Taubin asserts, and as von Trotta's subsequent works as a director illustrate, 'She brings a feminist and psychological perspective that complements Schlöndorff's Brechtian-styled political critique. Combining elements of melodrama and social satire, *Katharina Blum* is powerful to the degree that the acting is understated and the direction is supported by a nuanced sense of dramatic irony' (2003).

The first female director to win the Golden Lion at the Venice Film Festival for *The German Sisters* (*Die bleierne Zeit*) in 1981, Margarethe von Trotta is responsible for *The Second Awakening of Christa Klages* (*Das zweite Erwachen der Christa Klages*, 1978), *Sisters, or the Balance of Happiness* (*Schwestern oder Die Balance des Glücks*, 1979), *Sheer Madness* (*Heller Wahn*, 1983, and also featuring Winkler), *Rosa Luxemburg* (1986) and the more recent *Hannah Arendt* (2012, featuring Barbara Sukowa, the actor perhaps most synonymous with von Trotta), amongst many others. One of the most gifted – but often overlooked – directors to come from the New German Cinema movement, emerging at the same time as Rainer Werner Fassbinder, Werner Schroeter, Wim Wenders and Werner Herzog, von Trotta's achievement and place in film history have been recently celebrated both by HOME (as part of its *Celebrating Women in Global Cinema* project) and by the Independent Cinema Office with joint seasons titled *The Personal Is Political: The Films of Margaretha von Trotta*. Describing her as one of the world's leading feminist filmmakers, the Independent Cinema Office highlighted von Trotta's engagement with 'topics that resonated with contemporary lives and which prompt revolutionary discussions' (2019). Their website went on to state:

> The power of mass media, historical events, radicalisation and women's rights pre-#MeToo have all been visible elements in her films since the politically turbulent 1970s. Not to mention her wonderfully complex and outspoken female characters, precursors of those now taking centre stage in the best works by contemporary directors including Jane Campion, Andrea Arnold, Lone Scherfig and Desiree Akhavan.

2019

Strangely, von Trotta was known to later remark in some quarters that she never truly regarded *The Lost Honour of Katharina Blum* – one of the first true commercial successes of the New German Cinema – as one of her movies (perhaps because it was made in collaboration with Schlöndorff) and yet is imbued with the feminist perspective for which the director would later be celebrated. Much of the power of the film lies with the female gaze from which the narrative unfolds and the incredible central performance from Angela Winkler, who after emerging from theatre in the 1960s would go on to become one of Germany's most renowned actors. Describing her as Joan of Arc-like, Taubin roundly praises the anchoring contribution of Winkler:

> As eloquent in silence as in speech, she portrays Katharina as a woman of unusually strong convictions who values her right to make her own decisions about her life and, most particularly, about her sexuality. The men she encounters react to her sense of self-worth as a challenge to their masculinity. When she refuses to play their game, they become enraged and intent on destroying her. The one thing that can be counted on to unite the various men in this film across class and political lines is the need to keep women in a subservient position. In the eyes of the law, Katharina is guilty, first and foremost, of the crime of being a woman. That she's a woman who refuses to allow the patriarchy to determine her value compounds her guilt.

2003

In the choice of language, the subtitles consistently foreground patriarchy and denigration of women in society. The owner of a bar in which Blum worked describes her as 'stiff as a board; you couldn't even pinch her arse. A waitress should look like a whore.'

Blum, as the film progresses, regains the territory of language and asserts her autonomy and agency. Initially responding to Kommissar Beizmenne's barking of 'Did he fuck you?' in regard to her assignation with Ludwig, Blum responds 'I wouldn't use that word.' After refusing to acquiesce to an attempt at kindness from the Kommissar and an offer of food and drink seemingly straight from the good cop, bad cop manual, Blum instead asks to be placed in a cell alone and apart from her captors. Beizmenne is only too pleased to grant her her wish. Resisting pressure to sign a confession, Blum agrees only on condition that it reflects that the relationship between her and Ludwig was equal, saying 'Advances are a one-sided action. Tenderness comes from both parties.'

As well as offering an attempt to understand the actions and philosophy of the Red Army Faction and leftist groups, Böll's source novel also functioned as an effective page-turner that incorporated police reports and third-party accounts. Schlöndorff and von Trotta do something similar (though they radically depart from the book by having Blum's act of violence appear at the end rather than at the beginning, no doubt to contribute to the film's escalating tension and unease), adopting a chapter-like diary structure which mirrors the format of newspaper headlines, ensuring that in both style and content, *The Lost Honour of Katharina Blum* succeeds as a taut political conspiracy thriller with its bargaining, trade-offs, cells and interrogation sequences and trials in which power frequently changes hands. Characters, and this is certainly true of both Beizmenne and Tötges, are frequently duplicitous and untrustworthy, using means both fair and foul to meet their objectives and achieve their goals. Shot largely in steely and oppressive blues and greys, the characters are frequently presented in confined interior spaces to give a sense of imprisonment. Cinematographer Jost Vacano would go on to shoot Wolfgang Petersen's *Das Boot* (1981, and also featuring Prochnow), a submarine-set war drama that takes claustrophobia and enforced internment to almost unendurable levels.

The film, which will certainly also appeal to connoisseurs of 1970s architecture, fashion and German automobiles (various Porsches, including a vibrant green one Ludwig uses as a getaway vehicle, and a mustard yellow Mercedes-Benz feature), also pointedly uses the syntax of cinema to effectively convey the extent to which surveillance is beginning to mediate our lives and to suggest a climate of being watched and spied upon by the state. The opening sequence depicts an undercover policeman shadowing Ludwig with a 16mm camera, the film stock reverting to black and white to articulate what the policeman sees. Ludwig appears as if in the crosshairs of a rifle. We later see what appears to be recovered footage – again black and white – of the pursuit of Ludwig's getaway vehicle, a brief but bracing car chase that signals a further nod to thriller tropes. In this sense, the film has something in common with American conspiracy thrillers of the period such as Francis Ford Coppola's *The Conversation* and Alan J. Pakula's *The Parallax View* (both 1974), both of which in narrative terms look at Orwellian Big Brother ideologies that work to maintain positions of power at the expense of individual freedom. In terms of more recent European political thrillers, Florian Henckel von Donnersmarck's *The Lives of Others* (2006) bares traces of *The Lost Honour of Katharina Blum* in theme and execution.

The film's co-directors also anticipated the ways in which emerging technology would later come to be used, initially in the 1980s with video recorders by world cinema directors such as Atom Egoyan (*Family Viewing*, 1987, *The Adjuster*, 1991, *Calendar*, 1993), who from the outset of his career expressed a fascination with the increasing role recorded media would play in private and public life.

Upon its initial release, the film was not without its critics, as Taubin notes: 'Danièle Huillet, who, with her partner Jean-Marie Straub, made films that fall into the experimental end of the New German Cinema spectrum, criticised *Katharina Blum* when it was first released for employing a code of realism that, she claimed, would become incomprehensible in twenty years' (2003). However, for many, as Taubin asserts, 'Time has proven her wrong. In its mapping of tensions between the individual and a paranoid society, *The Lost Honor of Katharina* Blum is an utterly contemporary film' (2003). Rewatching the film again in a climate in which every act is recorded, magnified and commented upon and in which people lose their lives and their livelihoods through the act of shaming and a cacophony of virtual and actual abuse, it is hard to think of a film more on the money. What is perhaps most terrifying is how little we have learned. Similarly, the film offers an uncomfortable portrait of how the media and the government frequently collude in order to maintain an axis of power, manipulating facts to their own end to present a sanctioned view of acceptable behaviours and philosophies.

References

Elsaesser, T. (1989). *New German Cinema: A History*. New Brunswick: Rutgers University Press.

Independent Cinema Office (2019). 'The Personal Is Political – The Films of Margarethe von Trotta'. Retrieved from: www.independentcinemaoffice.org.uk/tours/margarethe-von-trotta/

Kieselbach, S. (2018, 8 October). 'Heinrich Böll: *The Lost Honour of Katharina Blum*'. *DW*. Retrieved from: www.dw.com/en/heinrich-b%C3%B6ll-the-lost-honour-of-katharina-blum/a-44527015

Taubin, A. (2003, 24 February). 'Honoring Katharina: *The Lost Honor of Katharina Blum*'. *Criterion*. Retrieved from: www.criterion.com/current/posts/1076-honoring-katharina-the-lost-honor-of-katharina-blum

12

Where the political thriller was less prevalent

Andy Willis

Figure 13 *Siete días de enero* (1979), courtesy of Mercury Video

In some countries during the 1970s, the political thriller did not seem to be as prevalent as it was in the major European film-producing countries such as France and Italy. This could simply have been due to the film industries of these countries, for example, the likes of Sweden, having a much smaller production infrastructure and output than those of France and Italy. Or, it could have been due to the fact that their film industries were experiencing a sharp reduction in output due to economic factors, as was the case in the United Kingdom. Another major factor in some countries not becoming associated with the form of the political thriller, even though it proved durable commercially, was that their industries had close associations with more dictatorial or totalitarian governments, as was the case in Spain. Whatever the reason for a smaller number of political thrillers emanating from these production contexts, interesting examples were produced during the decade, showing how the form could be manipulated to engage with a wide range of situations.

As Roy Stafford explores later in this dossier with regard to the Swedish film *Man on the Roof* (*Mannen på taket*, Bo Widerberg, 1976), there are some particularly notable examples of when the political thriller, even as a form not closely associated with the film industry of a particular country, has made a significant contribution to a national cinema. In this case, this was closely linked to both the reputation of the filmmaker, Bo Widerberg, and the writers of the source material, a novel called *The Abominable Man* by the highly influential crime writers Maj Sjöwall and Per Wahlöö. So, whilst Widerberg himself had already acquired an international reputation through films such as *Elvira Madigan* (1967) and *Joe Hill* (1971), when combined with the names of Sjöwall and Wahlöö, it became even more significant through its association with well-respected crime literature.

The UK was another location not associated with producing a great number of overtly political thrillers. However, the end of the 1970s did see a brief embracing of the form. Completed at the end of the decade and released in the early 1980s, *The Long Good Friday* (John Mackenzie, 1980) was probably the most effective at combining genre thrills with a political reflection on contemporary British society. Directed by John Mackenzie and written by Barrie Keeffe, the film revolves around a London gangster, Harold Shand, played by Bob Hoskins, who dreams of developing swathes of London's rundown dockland. As a result of this, he hopes to become a legitimate businessman and leave his past behind. Part of his strategy is to enter into a partnership with the American Mafia. Shand's commercial aspirations are clear precursors to the outlook of the new Conservative government that was elected in 1979 and its commitment to free-market economics. In this sense, Shand represents a type of new conservatism in the UK, which through his business ambitions is suggested by the film to be linked to gangsterism. When Shand's plans are put in jeopardy due to a number of his associates and properties being attacked, he becomes increasingly paranoid. As he sets out to discover who is behind the occurrences, the story begins to shift and he slowly realises the answer is much more political than he ever imagined. With its blending of the gangster film, the politics of inner-city renewal and political corruption, as well as its use of the Northern Irish Troubles as a backdrop, *The Long Good Friday* is a development in the concept of the political thriller, embracing the changing politics of the early 1980s and articulating their differences to those of the post-1968 era.

As noted above, other countries seem not to have embraced the form of the political thriller because of the socio-political context within which their film industry operated. In such cases, there are rare examples when directors attempted to take the thriller format and make some kind of political commentary. In the context of Europe, this is most obviously the case in countries where the ruling regime was more dictatorial and took close note of the output of the film industry. This is often most obvious through censorial practices which prevent certain content before production, through practices such as script approval or afterwards through the prevention of screenings or requests for content to be removed in order to achieve approval for release into cinemas. This would include countries that for some part of the 1970s were governed by dictatorships such as Portugal (until 1974), Spain (until 1975) and Greece (until 1974) or the countries that made up the bloc influenced by the Soviet Union in Eastern Europe. In these contexts, films that explored conspiracies involving official corruption, the linking of organised crime with government practices or the oppression of citizens by government agencies were not encouraged. The fact that all of these elements can be found in examples of the European political thriller explains why this form in particular was not commonly embraced by filmmakers in these countries, perhaps often practising some level of self-censorship.

In this section of the dossier, Eleftheria Rania Kosmidou explores an interesting example, the Greek film *Days of '36* (*Meres tou '36*, 1972). During the 1970s, its director Theo Angelopoulos had built a reputation for making films that were formally challenging and highly stylised. On this occasion, he chose to use the narrative conventions of the political thriller but to very different effect to the more popular films that were being made by the likes of Costa-Gavras and Elio Petri. In *Days of '36*, this takes the form of an imprisoned murderer taking a government official hostage in prison, which sparks a political crisis. Rather than the taut, exciting form of a conventional political thriller, *Days of '36* is full of Angelopoulos's trademark symmetrical compositions that whilst on paper may have the plot of a thriller, on screen displays the director's use of film form to resist the pleasures of commercial genre cinema.

Explored by Declan Clarke in another chapter in this dossier, the East German production *Die Flucht* (*The Flight*, 1977) is a rare example of a political thriller from Eastern Europe. Directed by Roland Gräf, a stalwart of the country's state-run production company DEFA (*Deutsche Film-Aktiengesellschaft*), and the final film made in East Germany by actor Armin Mueller-Stahl before he was blacklisted, *Die Flucht* won the Grand Prix at the Karlovy Vary International Film Festival in 1978. The film focuses on the story of a doctor, Schmith, who dutifully follows procedure in his application to travel outside the German Democratic Republic (GDR) to attend a conference, yet is refused permission. Dismayed by the state bureaucracy, he becomes involved with an underground network who promise they can get him out of the country. Given it was made in the East, it is perhaps not surprising all does not go to plan as the filmmakers use the form of the thriller to explore agencies that helped people try to escape to the West.

Both *Days of '36* and *The Flight* are films that attempt to engage with the form of the political thriller in contexts that due to the specificity of local politics are in some way surprising. In these examples, this leads to a rather oblique use of some of the codes and conventions of the thriller as filmmakers combine them with aspects of the art film and the melodrama respectively. Fraser Elliott's contribution focuses on a more mainstream political thriller, the Spanish–Italian co-production *Ogre* (1979). In this instance, the particularly Spanish subject of Basque terrorism was one that could only be addressed following the death of the dictator General Franco in November 1975. Influential Italian director Gillo Pontecorvo, who had made his name as a political filmmaker with *The Battle of Algiers* in 1966, made a political thriller, released in 1979 in Italy and known in Spain, where it was released in 1980, as *Operación Ogro*, that recreates the assassination of Admiral Carrero Blanco in 1973 by an ETA (*Euskadi Ta Askatasuna* – Basque Homeland and

Liberty) cell. The film stars the stalwart of the political thriller, Gian Maria Volonté, alongside Spanish actors such as Eusebio Poncela and Ángela Molina. It certainly fits the category of the European political thriller as it is marked by scenes of taut dramatic tension as the cell plan and carry out their assassination, and then make good their escape through the crowded city of Madrid. *Ogre* was one of a number of notable political thrillers made in Spain towards the end of the 1970s, and I now want to explore some of these and offer a case study of Spain as an example of a place where the political thriller was less prevalent but where it did manage to engage with the politics of the Spanish transition from dictatorship to democracy at the end of the decade.

Spain after Franco

Whilst much of Europe had begun to produce films that broadly responded to particular socio-political circumstances through the flexible form of the thriller in the early 1970s, Spain, under the dictatorship of General Franco, offered very few examples until the decade was reaching its end. Strict censorship had meant that those filmmakers seeking to offer critiques of the regime worked in less direct, more obliquely allegorical modes such as Víctor Erice's acclaimed *Spirit of the Beehive* (*El espíritu de la colmena*, 1973). Others, like Vicente Aranda with *The Blood Spattered Bride* (*La Novia Ensangrentada*, 1972), immersed themselves in commercial genres such as the horror film.

One rare example of a Spanish political thriller from this period is José Louis Borau's *B Must Die* (*Hay que matar a B.*, 1974), a work that Marsha Kinder has described as having 'a complex plot evocative of both Lang and Hitchcock' (1993: 348) and of being a 'politicized noir thriller' (352). In the 1960s, Borau had worked on documentary shorts and genre films such as the western *Ride and Kill* (*Brandy/Cavalca e uccidi*, 1964), the crime film *Double Edged Crime* (*Crimen de doble filo*, 1965) and produced the musical comedy *Un, dos, tres ... al escondite inglés* (1970). Originally, *B Must Die* was set in the Basque country, but at the script stage, censors had forced the filmmakers to relocate the setting to an unnamed Latin American country (Hopewell, 1986: 100).

When it finally went into production, *B Must Die* was shot in English with American actors Darren McGavin, Patricia Neal and Burgess Meredith cast alongside French performer Stéphane Audran. The film is set in a fictitious, repressive South American dictatorship that can still easily be read as commenting on Spain's internal politics. As Hopewell observed, 'Scripted in 1966 ... *Hay que matar a B.* reflects a common concern of Spanish cinema in the 60s: a call for collective action, for new political consciousness in self-satisfied Spaniards' (1986: 99). Whilst a misguided Pal, a Hungarian immigrant played by McGavin, thinks he is above the everyday politics of a country that is not his own, the film slowly reveals that he is as manipulated by the dictatorship as much as anyone else. As Hopewell sums it up, 'the source of both private and public discontent is the same – the country's present political regime' (1986: 99). Hopewell's response is also telling in regard to how Borau was attempting to use the format of the thriller for political ends but also how the form could lead to misinterpretation of that politics. He argues that 'Critical reaction to Borau's film was that it was not particularly original variation on the theme of an individual victimized by the secret state. Yet it was designed to be exactly the opposite' (1986: 99). It would seem to me that the success of the latter would be dependent upon the type of state that is created. Here, its dictatorial nature is central to making this a film to stand alongside the other political thrillers produced across Europe by the likes of Costa-Gavras, Petri and Rosi.

With the death of the Spanish dictator in 1975 and the lifting of censorship in 1977, Spanish filmmakers were able to embrace more directly the idea of the political thriller. Juan Antonio Bardem, long an opponent of the dictatorship and a member of the PCE, the Spanish Communist Party, was one of those who chose to do so. Bardem had previously been imprisoned for his opposition to the Franco dictatorship. In her biography, blacklisted Hollywood actress Betsy Blair describes how during the shooting of Bardem's *Calle Major* (*Main Street*, 1956), in which she played the lead, production was stopped due to the director being arrested. She recalls how producer Manuel J. Goyanes met her at her hotel one morning stating that 'We won't be shooting tomorrow – Juan Antonio has been arrested' (2003: 269). The director was released and the film completed, but the incident reflects the precarious existence of opposition filmmakers and perhaps explains, along with the censorship regime in operation, why direct critiques of the Franco political system were rare.

When things changed after Franco's death, Bardem was one of those filmmakers who utilised the form of the political thriller. He did so most notably with *Seven Days in January* (*Siete días de enero*, 1979), a film made as a direct retort to the murder of a group of left-wing activists at a legal support office by a right-wing death squad in the Atocha area of Madrid on 24 January 1977. Bardem responded quickly to the murders by making a taut, complex, documentary-style thriller that recreated these events in detail. It proposed the idea that the killings were part of a wider rightwing move to create a state of political tension in Spain that would lead to calls for a return to dictatorship. The tactic, similar to that shown in Italian films such as *Illustrious Corpses* (1976), is explored through showing a web of conspiracies and clandestine activities orchestrated by the right, whilst the film clearly combines fiction, in the offering of a backstory for the assassins and the creation of the tension so important within the political thriller, with the near documentary creation of the political response to the killings in the form of demonstrations, and the police's clampdown on any street protests following the killings. For John Hopewell, these two elements did not gel, with him being unconvinced by the more dramatic elements of the film such as the use of slow motion and the choice of music to accompany shots of the funeral (1986: 108–109). However, forty plus years later, and in the context of *States of Danger and Deceit*, the film and its thesis of a strategy of tension within the context of Spain in the late 1970s certainly compares well to the work of Francesco Rosi in Italy.

At the end of the 1970s, Eloy de la Iglesia, another Spanish director with links to the country's PCE, embarked upon a series of urgent films that blended the more melodramatic tendencies of popular cinema with subjects drawn from the social and political issues facing contemporary Spain. These included a series of films that explored the figure of the juvenile delinquent: *Navajeros* (1981), *Colegas* (1982), *El Pico* (1983) and *El Pico II* (1984). De la Iglesia had built a reputation earlier in the 1970s for working sociopolitical themes into his popular genre films such as the psychological thrillers *The Glass Ceiling* (*El techo de cristal*, 1971) and *No*

One Heard the Scream (*Nadie oyó gritar*, 1973), the social realist horror film *Cannibal Man* (*La semana del asesino*, 1972) and the science fiction-themed *Murder in a Blue World* (*Una gota de sangre para morir amando*, 1973). By the end of the decade, he could be more direct in his tackling political subjects. John Hopewell variously describes his post-Franco work as 'violent social protest films', 'social melodrama', 'family drama' and 'rampant melodrama' (1986: 221–222). These films were an attempt to directly address the urgency of the politics of the day. As Paul Julian Smith notes, quoting a 1983 interview with the director, 'de la Iglesia himself called for a cinema that would be "like a newspaper"'. And that 'it is impossible to consider his films outside the immediate context of the transition to democracy' (1998: 217). In evoking the idea of films quite literally grabbed from the headlines, Smith goes on to argue that this 'suggests political engagement: the film will not flinch from editorializing, from making wholly explicit its political bias' (1998: 217). *The Deputy* (*El diputado*, 1978), one of the key works De la Iglesia directed in this period, blends his melodramatic tendencies with a plot that utilises the form of the political thriller. *The Deputy* explores the ways in which the political and the personal overlap as a gay Communist Party candidate realises that his relationship with a young juvenile delinquent potentially opens him up to blackmail from the forces of the right still active in the shadows. De la Iglesia followed this with a series of films that again combined elements of the thriller with the social melodrama in their representation of the margins of Spanish society.

The identification of *Seven Days in January* and *The Deputy* as being in the tradition of the European political thriller of the 1970s opens up the potential to draw in other Spanish crime films of the period into the category. This highlights the political motivation behind the films and their adoption of a more commercial film form and links them to other work produced across the continent in the period of the Spanish transition to democracy. These include works that use their conspiracy plotlines and representation of corrupt officialdom to address the legacy of Franco's authoritarian government in the post-dictatorship period. The most obvious candidate for this is *Con uñas y dientes* (*Tooth and Nail*, Paulino Viota, 1978). This film's conspiracy narrative revolves around a trade unionist who uncovers corruption amongst management but ends up dead before he can reveal the truth. In the end, the old management regime is replaced by a slightly more liberal one, the system remaining safely in place. A film of the immediate post-Franco era, it is described by Hopewell as being 'part thriller, part detective story, part softcore movie'. He goes on to suggest that director Paulino Viota also works to subvert the styles that he utilises, creating, like the best European political thrillers, a rather sophisticated piece of work (1986: 220).

Whilst the 1970s had not seen many political thrillers produced in Spain, the coming decades would see a number of filmmakers turn to the form to explore their current political situations in a manner championed by filmmakers across Europe in that decade. As with the 1970s, some of these were driven by political conviction, whilst others used politics and the misbehaviour of agencies of the state as a backdrop designed for commercial appeal. These films and filmmakers form part of the legacy of the European political thriller which will be explored further at the end of this dossier.

References

Blair, B. (2003). *The Memory of All That: Love and Politics in New York, Hollywood and Paris*. New York: Alfred A. Knopf.

Hopewell, J. (1986). *Out of the Past: Spanish Cinema after Franco*. London: British Film Institute.

Kinder, M. (1993). *Blood Cinema: The Reconstruction of National Identity in Spain*. Berkeley: University of California Press.

Smith, P. J. (1998). 'Homosexuality, Regionalism, and Mass Culture: Eloy de la Iglesia's Cinema of Transition'. In J. Talens and S. Zunzunegui (Eds), *Modes of Representation in Spanish Cinema*. Minneapolis: University of Minnesota Press, 216–251.

13

Operación Ogro (*Ogro*), Gillo Pontecorvo, 1979

Fraser Elliott

Figure 14 *Operación Ogro* (1979), courtesy of Cristaldi Film

On 20 December 1973, members of the Basque separatist group ETA (*Euskadi Ta Askatasuna* – Basque Homeland and Freedom) assassinated the Spanish Prime Minister, Luis Carrero Blanco. A staunch supporter of the dictatorship that had been in power since the end of the Civil War in 1939, Carrero Blanco had been set to replace head of state General Francisco Franco, whose health was in rapid decline by the early 1970s, and take control of the Spanish state. Aside from its political importance and social implications, Blanco's murder was widely acknowledged at the time for the uniqueness of ETA's method and the peculiarity of how it unfolded. After nearly five months of preparation, digging underneath Calle Claudio Coello, a street in the Salamanca district of Madrid, the ETA commando unit detonated eighty kilograms worth of explosives as Blanco drove by in his Dodge Dart. The explosion was so powerful that the vehicle was launched over twenty metres into the air, over rooftops, before landing on a terrace on an adjacent road. The attempt was successful and Blanco died shortly thereafter in hospital.

These are the events covered in detail in the 1979 political thriller *Operación Ogro*, directed by the Italian Gillo Pontecorvo, which shares its name with that given to the assassination plot by ETA. Whilst it may seem unfair to include the result of the assassination attempt in the first paragraph of an introduction to the film, it is important because the assumed knowledge in the viewer is one of the areas that makes this European political thriller so interesting and unlike its contemporaries. Unusual for a film in this genre – based on political intrigue and the fraught potential of failure (with serious repercussions) for an assassination attempt – the notoriety of Blanco's assassination means that most of the audiences who saw *Operación Ogro* at the time of its release would have been intimately familiar with its conclusion before seeing even the opening credits. In fact, the original Spanish poster for the film is simply an image of Blanco's car mid-flight following the explosion.

Partly as a result of this ubiquity, far from being a strict genre piece, *Operación Ogro* exists as a complex collection of seemingly conflicting ambitions and realisations. On the one hand, it functions as a tense thriller, one whose set pieces succeed even to a viewer who knows their outcome ahead of time. On the other, however, it repeatedly undercuts this tension and uses the case study of Blanco's assassination to ask probing questions about the utility and morality of political violence as a tool. It is a film whose genre commitments are compromised by an anxious meditation on the part of its director who seeks to problematise and complicate the morality and function of the violent events presented on screen. *Operación Ogro* and its grounding in actual historical events represent well a tension in European political thrillers of the 1970s between their commitment to genre and the real-world settings of their stories.

Operación Ogro is composed of two interweaving narratives, rare in that they are told from the terrorists' point of view.

The first covers the planning, plotting and execution of the 1973 assassination. This narrative arc contains the film's most generic plot characteristics: meetings at which the plans are finalised; reconnaissance work as the group observe Blanco's routine around his daily church visits; the slow dig underneath Calle Claudio Coello and the risk of discovery from neighbours and local police; and, eventually, a tense, drawn-out scene of the assassination itself, complete with ambitious and bombastic special effects. The second arc contains much of the political context and messaging of the film, told through flashbacks to the group's childhood and Basque education and flashforwards as the fractured group witness Spain's transition to democracy at the end of the decade. The viewer is guided through these interwoven events principally via the friendship and philosophical tension between Ezarra and Txabi, whose political disagreements offer multiple viewpoints and ways to make sense of the unfolding violence. Ezarra believes that patience and long-term planning are the best routes to meaningful structural political change, whilst Txabi subscribes to a more urgent rhetoric of immediate, violent action and fast results. The disagreements of these men and their comrades are one of the principal ways *Operación Ogro* offers a contemplation on the morality of political violence that was still relevant to an audience in late-1970s and early-1980s Europe. Not contained to the Spain of 1973 depicted on screen, these viewpoints informed events, like the fascist bombing of Bologna Centrale railway station in 1980, that would have been fresh in the minds of its contemporary viewers.

Ezarra and Txabi are played by the Italian Gian Maria Volonté and the Spaniard Eusebio Poncela respectively, starring roles that are indicative of *Operación Ogro*'s status as a Spanish–Italian co-production, and they bring to the film their own political associations for various viewers at different times. Volonté, for example, was well known for his outspoken left-wing leanings and public comments and recognised within Italy for his roles in politically engaged dramas from leftist directors such as Elio Petri and Francesco Rosi. These included *Investigation of a Citizen above Suspicion* (Elio Petri, 1970), *The Mattei Affair* (Francesco Rosi, 1972) and *Lucky Luciano* (Francesco Rosi, 1973). He perhaps remains most recognisable to international viewers for his appearances in spaghetti westerns from Sergio Leone's *Dollars*

Trilogy (1964–1966) to *A Bullet for the General* (Damiano Damiani, 1966). His co-star, Poncela, had made a name for himself in films now considered 'cult' classics including Eloy de la Inglesia's *The Cannibal Man* (1972), a Spanish horror film that made it on to Britain's Director of Public Prosecutions list of 'video nasties' in 1983. However, in Spain, he was also a noted figure around the time of *Operación Ogro*'s release for his roles in challenging films like *Arrebato* (*Rapture*, Iván Zulueta, 1980), now seen as a key work of *La Movida*, the Madrid-based artistic movement that emerged during Spain's transition to democracy in the late 1970s and early 1980s. Alongside these men, the cast is filled with numerous actors from across these regional industries including the Spaniard Ángela Molina, at the time best known internationally for *That Obscure Object of Desire* (Luis Buñuel, 1977), and Italian Saverio Marconi, who had established himself internationally with *Padre Padrone* (Paolo and Vittorio Taviani, 1977), whose inclusion further points towards the film's transnational production status and would assist its marketing in each country.

Despite its specific grounding in Spanish politics and the local historical moment of Blanco's death, Italy looms large over *Operación Ogro*, from its Italian stars to a soundtrack created by noted Italian composer Ennio Morricone, direction from Pontecorvo and an Italian edit of the film which, dubbed in Italian and retitled simply *Ogro*, included an additional introductory sequence detailing the historical context of Spanish politics and the Basque desire for independence. This Italian version was the print chosen by the programming team at HOME for its screening in the *States of Danger and Deceit* season because the historical context of the Basque struggle it presents proved equally useful for a 2017 UK audience as it was for an Italian one in 1979 when the film opened there. It is hard to imagine what *Operación Ogro* would look like without the significant creative contribution of the Italian practitioners involved, but it is worth noting that this specific regional pairing was not the original plan for the film.

Pontecorvo had been keen to make a film about Blanco's assassination from much earlier in the decade and had originally secured support from American studios to help in its production. United Artists, who had distributed Pontecorvo's earlier film *Burn!* (1969) throughout Europe, were attached to the project for close to two years. However, in a theme that defines much of *Operación Ogro*'s existence, the studio pulled out due to fears that the subject matter may prove controversial amongst the Francoists who remained influential within the Spanish government (Lucas, 1983). The resulting, final collaboration between Italian and Spanish production companies ultimately dictated a great deal of *Operación Ogro*'s final realisation, as noted above, but the importance of Italy – particularly the Italian political landscape in the second half of the 1970s – goes further than the inclusion of certain stars and an additional introduction. In fact, the entire political ambition of the film, and in turn the decisions to make it an interweaving narrative filled with contrasting ethical and philosophical possibilities, resulted from Pontecorvo's positioning in Italy and the effects of ongoing controversies there at the time.

One of only a handful of fiction films made across his fifty-year career, *Operación Ogro* was the final feature directed by Pontecorvo and the only film he made in the 1970s. On paper, it follows quite closely the subjects of his earlier films. In its fascination with guerrilla strategy and organised resistance, *Operación Ogro* shares themes with *Burn!*, a film about a slave revolt on a Caribbean island, and, notably, *The Battle of Algiers* (1966), a complex portrayal of Algerian resistance against the colonial French government. *The Battle of Algiers* remains the film that Pontecorvo is best remembered for. It is a polemic work, one that, according to Thomas Riegler, 'rationalises the use of violence as a political tool' (2009: 57). Although it details the effects of such violence for people on both sides of the struggle, this 1966 film has a confidence in its argumentation and realisation that suggests a director with clarity of thought about the utility of these methods in instigating political change. Whilst similar in theme, this is a confidence that is hard to find in *Operación Ogro*, which instead reveals Pontecorvo's growing anxieties around the moral justifications for political violence.

Much has been made of this transition in Pontecorvo's personal philosophy as a defining characteristic in the progression of his filmmaking career. Carlo Celli's monograph on the director, one of the only book-length studies of his films, is simply titled *From Resistance to Terrorism*, indicating the importance of this transformation in how Pontecorvo's work is understood.

Celli (2004a: 227) credits this transformation, in part, to political events in late-1970s Italy. Just as United Artists pulled out of the film due to fears or repercussions with the Spanish government, Pontecorvo had delayed production of the film from its original conception in 1976 to later in the decade because he was worried how the themes of political violence would resonate within his native Italy. The crux of his anxieties was the kidnapping of Aldo Moro, a centre-left politician and, at various times across his life, Prime Minister of Italy. Moro was kidnapped in 1978 by the far-left terrorist group *Brigate Rosse* (Red Brigades), and, after repeated threats and refusals to negotiate from the Italian government, was executed on 9 May of the same year. This act of political violence, undertaken not during a dictatorial regime but during a time of democratically elected, if imperfect, governance, clearly had an effect on Pontecorvo and his convictions in making a film told from the point of view of terrorists about a seemingly clear-cut instance of necessary and justified action. Partially as a result of these actions, as Celli notes, by the end of the 1970s, for those like Pontecorvo, 'the idea of ideologically driven violent struggle simply lost currency in Italy' (2004a: 227). In fact, Pontecorvo himself has commented that the film was 'made with a guilty conscience' following the events of Moro's kidnapping and murder (Celli, 2004b: 51).

Great efforts were evidently made by Pontecorvo to ensure the audience understood that the acts of terrorism displayed on screen in his film were 'justifiable under fascism, but erroneous today' (Riegler, 2009: 58). There are numerous characteristics that point towards this anxiety which end up creating a political thriller that often, quite strangely, seems to intentionally undercut its 'thrilling' moments, making it unique amongst its contemporaries in the genre discussed elsewhere in this collection. Whilst other political thrillers of the 1970s use terrorism and political resistance as a platform from which to tell their otherwise thrilling and fictional narratives, such as *The Lost Honour of Katharina Blum* (Volker Schlöndorff and Margarethe von Trotta, 1975) or *Knife in the Head* (Reinhard Hauff, 1978), *Operación Ogro*'s tense creep towards the execution of a complex assassination plot is repeatedly undermined by Pontecorvo's anxieties around its political context.

At times, within individual scenes, tension is certainly achieved through established genre tropes of the thriller. This is clearest in the film's tense recreation of the morning of Blanco's assassination that takes up close to twenty minutes of the film's 100-minute runtime. Numerous narrative threads resolve in this scene, but all have the potential to go wrong, to lead to the failure of the plot and the apprehension of Ezarra, Txabi and their colleagues. The fragility of these various links in the chain is emphasised through a collection of generic, formal characteristics: Morricone's sparse and brooding score includes an increasingly loud ticking sound as Blanco's car approaches the explosives; shots alternate between unsettling stationary cameras and those shakily mounted cars which vibrate and rattle as the team escape the scene of the crime; shot length is short and editing more frequent than elsewhere in the film; and fear of their capture escalates as a panicked radio announcer frantically shouts about the unfolding events on a distorted car radio. These formal characteristics are effective and can certainly work to elicit an appropriately heightened response in the viewer, but they only function this way when taken in isolation.

Any growing sense of tension and excitement throughout the narrative as a whole is repeatedly complicated, and in some ways intentionally weakened, by its form and narrative structure. There are the flashbacks and flashforwards that create a jumbled chronological structure, reducing tension but offering counterpoints to the promotion of terrorism as a political tool. The most prominent of these follows Txabi in 1978 as he is hospitalised from a gunshot wound, received when attempting to kill two police officers in the street. Scenes of the shooting, Txabi's hospitalisation and the beginnings of a conversation with Ezarra and the others are all intercut with the build-up and aftermath of Blanco's assassination, reducing tension as they appear. Elsewhere, there is a brief side-plot about enlisting construction workers by helping them unionise and strike – which only tangentially fits into the preparation and delivery of the unfolding assassination – and there are more minor scenes of disagreements within the group as they decide on their strategy for Blanco. Formally, these scenes all conform to a kind of 1970s realist, dialogue-driven drama: long takes with infrequent editing, mostly composed of two shots in medium close up, focusing on dialogue with no orchestrated score. It appears as though the filmmaking team seem less interested in incorporating these moments into a tense narrative and, instead, more compelled to complicate any easy interpretation of the political message potentially offered by the film. Its structure shows that problematising the events and viewpoints shown on screen is as important to Pontecorvo as faithfully recreating the 'official' version of events that unfolded in what was originally thought to be a decisively moral act.

Whilst *Operación Ogro* could be seen as a confused film, unsure of whether it wants to be a nail-biting tense thriller or a forum for contrasting viewpoints, acknowledging the context of Moro's assassination and the anxieties around political violence it catalysed in Pontecorvo suggests that this contradiction was an intended goal of the film. Although, as noted above, Pontecorvo openly discussed the ways in which acts of terrorism were justifiable during fascism but not during a more democratic context, the film itself is never as confident or convincing, showing instead evidence of the director's 'guilty conscience' and his personal redressing of earlier convictions.

These anxieties all inform the closing moments of *Operación Ogro* and the flashforward to 1978 and the hospital deathbed of Txabi as he is visited by Ezarra and others, years after they had successfully assassinated Blanco. Upon his arrival at the hospital, Ezarra is asked by a reporter how he feels about the actions of his former comrade. In an entirely unambiguous reply, Ezarra states: 'We used the armed struggle against fascism because we had no other means. Now it's different. Democracy, though fragile and incomplete, allows us to use other weapons.' He acknowledges that they can now 'circulate ideas', suggesting the need for the Basque community to work with the Spanish government peacefully to enact change in policy and institutions. Txabi, too, receives this kind of assurance from Ezarra. He asks: 'You've come to tell me I was right?', to which Ezarra shakes his head. Txabi replies 'Only with patience like yours can the world be changed', and Ezarra nods. Whilst the sincerity of Txabi in this moment is debatable, that of the film's director and his own crisis of confidence is clear.

This scene was written in a late redrafting of the script, added by Pontecorvo as a newly conceived ending intended to offer a more blanket dismissal of political violence following Moro's murder. It emphasises Pontecorvo's final intentions in *Operación Ogro* to explicitly denounce the acts of terrorism displayed on screen in the film and, to some extent, in the productions he made in decades prior. Any original intentions from Pontecorvo to promote, or at least sympathetically discuss, a potentially understandable act of anti-fascist resistance from an earlier era was untenable, personally and politically, when it came to realising the film in its final form. As a result, *Operación Ogro* stands as a unique production amidst its European contemporaries of the 1970s: a political thriller made somewhat less thrilling for its politics but one that remains a fascinating example of a genre film with a complex relationship to the political contexts of both its chosen subject and its era of production.

References

Celli, C. (2004a). 'Aldo Vergano's IL SOLE SORGE ANCORA/OUTCRY (1946) as Influence on Gillo Pontecorvo'. *Forum Italicum*, 38(1), 217–228.
Celli, C. (2004b). 'Gillo Pontecorvo's Return to Algiers'. *Film Quarterly*, 58(2), 49–52.
Lucas, C. (1983). 'Interview with Gillo Pontecorvo'. In D. Georgakas and L. Rubenstein (Eds), *The Cineaste Interviews on the Art and Politics of the Cinema*. Chicago: Lake View Press, 307–312.
Riegler, T. (2009). 'Gillo Pontecorvo's "Dictatorship of Truth" – A Legacy'. *Studies in European Cinema*, 6(1), 47–62.

14

Die Flucht (*The Flight*), Roland Gräf, 1977

Declan Clarke

Figure 15 *Die Flucht* (1977), courtesy of Berlin DEFA Foundation

Die Flucht is an unusual film, made at an unusual time, in an unusual place, under unusual circumstances. An unusual film in that it is about a successful doctor who is looking to flee the German Democratic Republic (GDR) to begin a new life in West Germany, and made at an unusual time because in the late 1970s, Warsaw Pact countries tended not to make films about the potential failings of their own political systems. From a contemporary perspective, this made East Germany possibly the last place one would expect such a film to be made.

The 1970s in the GDR were rather different to the late 1980s when the country was sliding towards extinction. In fact, the 1970s were different across Central and Eastern Europe in a manner that is rarely considered in retrospect. It was a period when Erich Honecker was viewed as a liberal, moderate voice by the West, having replaced Walther Ulbricht as General Secretary of the *Sozialistische Einheitspartei Deutschlands* (SED, Socialist Unity Party of Germany) in May 1971. His Romanian counterpart, Nicolae Ceaușescu, was similarly viewed; successive US Presidents Nixon and Ford had been to visit Romania, each hoping it could be turned into an ally against the Soviet Union were a third global conflict to break out. Ceaușescu himself made four state visits to the US. Alexander Dubček's Prague Spring may have been crushed in May 1968 by the Soviet Union, acting under the auspices of the Warsaw Pact Alliance (the communist counterpart set up after the founding of NATO to guard against and counteract the stated aims of the latter), and Czechoslovakia was under a process of 'normalisation' under Gustáv Husák. In Poland, Edward Gierek had replaced Władysław Gomłka as First Secretary of the Polish United Workers' Party at the close of 1970, after a wave of strikes and protests against the rising costs of living essentials had been harshly and violently suppressed under Gomłka's direction. Although Gierek was only eight years younger than the sixty-five-year-old he usurped, across communist Europe, there was a sense of transition and liberalisation, the impression that perhaps the single party state leaders were willing to listen to the people and adapt to the cultural changes that had emerged during the 1960s. Together, these gave the impression that Eastern Bloc countries had got over the shock of both the uprisings and their subsequent suppressions and were easing towards a more moderate and less overtly Stalinist approach.

In contrast, as the 1970s got under way, the West seemed to be falling apart. Greece was under the grip of successive (CIA-backed) military coups d'état, as was Turkey. Spain and Portugal still had fascist dictatorships in place; Italy was in the throes of the *anni di piombo* (as discussed elsewhere in this collection); in the UK, Edward Heath had introduced the Three-Day Week in response to the 1973–1974 oil crisis, and the Troubles in Northern Ireland had commenced; France was reeling from a wave of strikes that had ground the economy to a standstill, as the fallout from the events of May 1968 gave many Western observers a genuine fear that both France and Italy could fall to democratically elected communism. The United States was suffering from a stagnant economy and seemed to be lurching from crisis to crisis as it attempted to win an unwinnable war in Vietnam. Add to this regular hijackings, Carlos 'The Jackal' laying siege to the OPEC headquarters in Vienna, holding thirty-six people hostage (and killing three) whilst still making off with the ransom, and the relative calm that seemed to be emanating from the post-Stalinist thaw in Eastern Bloc nations seemed almost soothing in comparison.

By the early 1970s, the state film studios of the GDR, DEFA (*Deutsche Film-Aktiengesellschaft*), was also going through a renaissance as the influence of the cinematic New Wave movements, spearheaded by the French *nouvelle vague*, that were emerging throughout both East and West Europe found directors making more topical films that dealt with contemporary themes, as opposed to reflecting on the post-war fallout and the building of socialism. In part, these were influenced by changing trends beyond the East German border and a desire for East Germany to produce a simulacrum of contemporary Western trends that still adhered to the values of socialism or at the very least underlined the failings of capitalism. Cinema in the GDR had always been a popular recreational pursuit. Prior to the installation of the Berlin Wall in 1961, approximately 25,000 people daily crossed the East Berlin–West Berlin border to view films in the 'border theatres' in 1956–1957 (Fulbrook, 2005: 74). Once these cross-border visits were unable to continue, censorship played a more increasing restriction on cinema, culminating in the notoriously restrictive Eleventh Plenum of December 1965 in which eleven films were banned. Plenary sessions were political administrative meetings in which the SED would meet to agree economic, political, cultural and social strategies going forward. The Eleventh Plenum was notable as its central focus emerged as being a discussion on youth and culture and the perception that a void had been created that exposed young people to malign 'outside' influence.

Two films were screened at the Plenum: *Berlin um die Ecke* (*Berlin around the Corner*, Gerhard Klein, 1965), which was deemed 'dishonest and anti-socialist', and *Das Kaninchen bin ich*

(*I Am the Rabbit*, Kurt Maetzig, 1965), which was considered an attack on the judicial system. Both were promptly banned. *Berlin um die Ecke* and *Das Kaninchen bin ich* were representative of the emerging *Alltag* (Everyday) movement, comparative to other European New Wave movements or the kitchen sink realism equivalent that emerged out of the Free Cinema movement in the UK. An irony worth noting here is that the latter films were criticised for advocating a socialist perspective in the UK, whilst the former films were censored for not sufficiently advocating the right kind of socialist perspective in the GDR. Nine other films not screened at the Plenum were banned and a sense of a new wave of cultural restriction loomed.

The Eleventh Plenum was the culmination of a desire to curb the burgeoning youth culture that was growing during the mid-1960s in the GDR. The most significant measure taken against it by authorities was the *Beatverbot* ('Beat-Ban') in Leipzig, where forty-four of the forty-nine bands performing on the city circuit were banned from playing, thus leading to demonstrations on 30–31 October 1965. Around 2,500 people congregated in the city centre, and heavy-handed policing, that included the use of water cannons and truncheon runs, saw 267 young people arrested, many of whom were given punitive spells in work camps as a result. The echoes between the Leipzig *Beatverbot* of 1965 and the Munich *Schwabinger Krawalle* (Schawbinger riots) of 1962 are noteworthy. In the latter, a band of street musicians played beyond the 10:30 p.m. curfew, prompting an excessive response by the Munich police when they tried to forcefully arrest the musicians and thus unleashed a four-day street battle with approximately 40,000 students, 400 of whom were arrested, with many imprisoned. Andreas Baader, co-founder of the *Rote Armee Fraktion* (Red Army Faction), or Baader-Meinhof Group, would later cite it as the formative moment of his political awakening (Kalb, 2020: 168).

Explaining the reasoning behind the censorship of culture at the Eleventh Plenum, Erich Honecker stated: 'The matter is quite straightforward. If we are to increase productivity – and thereby raise our standard of living still further – we cannot afford to propagate nihilistic, defeatist and immoral philosophies in literature, film, drama and television. Scepticism and a rising standard of living are ... mutually incompatible' (in Allan and Sandford, 1999: 13). The push against youth culture was spearheaded by Honecker, which made it both surprising and ominous that he would emerge as the liberal voice when he replaced Walther Ulbricht. Upon ascending the presidency a few years later, he ignited a 'no taboo' policy alongside a programme of liberalisation. This in effect reversed the Eleventh Plenum restrictions that led to a spate of more socially topical films. Honecker's statement on the matter was: 'Providing one starts from an established socialist standpoint, there cannot, in my opinion, be any taboo subjects for art and literature' (Allan and Sandford, 1999: 14). So, a freedom of sorts rather than a freedom absolute.

The most significant of the taboo-breaking films that emerged in this period of liberalisation was Heiner Carow's *Die Legende von Paul und Paula* (*The Legend of Paul and Paula*, 1973). The film is now seen as a cult classic of Central European cinema and could be called a quasi-counterculture melodrama. It has more in common with the melodramas that Rainer Werner Fassbinder was making in West Germany around the same time than it does *Easy Rider* (Dennis Hopper, 1969), or *Blow-Up* (Michelangelo Antonioni, 1966), but it had and maintains a comparative impact on the culture. A tragic, and at times surreal, film, *Die Legende von Paul und Paula* paved the way for a more contemporary issue-conscious cinema in the GDR. Though censors wanted to ban the film, Erich Honecker personally recommended its release.

Erich Honecker was sixty-five when *Die Flucht* was released four years later, and despite its eyebrow-raising theme – fleeing the People's Republic – the film was not censored or restricted. As Fulbrook (2005) notes, at the time, young people made up the overwhelming majority of film audiences, with the average age of a filmgoer being twenty-four, interestingly, the precise average age of the people who sought to flee west. Significantly, film audiences in the GDR at this time did not have to rely on a steady diet of East German or indeed Eastern Bloc films, with many Western films being the most popular with audiences by a considerable margin. Listed amongst the most-watched films in terms of attendance figures were *The Towering Inferno* (John Guillermin, 1974), which was popular with mainstream audiences, and *One Flew over the Cuckoo's Nest* (Milos Forman, 1975), which proved successful with the intelligentsia (Fulbrook, 2005: 75).

Another interesting feature of *Die Flucht* is that, even though it addresses an illegal though relatively commonplace activity, the Stasi (the *Staatssicherheitsdienst* or State Security Service) have only a superficial role. Though clearly a menacing presence to Schmith when they are investigating Dr Wendt's attempt to abscond west, this is largely due to the paranoia Schmith feels with regard to his own imminent departure. It is now almost impossible to see a filmed representation of the GDR that not only features the Stasi prominently but features them as a central character, story arc or theme, from the more balanced and meritorious *Good Bye Lenin!* (Wolfgang Becker, 2003) or *Barbara* (Christian Petzold, 2012) to the clichéd *Sonnenallee* (Leander Haußmann, 1999) or *Das Leben der Anderen* (*The Lives of Others*, Florian Henckel von Donnersmarck, 2006). Even the recently celebrated television series *Deutschland '83* (2015) is set wholly within the confines of the *Ministerium für Staatssicherheit*. Comparatively, this is not true in the case of depictions of the era in the former Soviet Union, Hungary, Czech Republic/Slovakia, Romania or Poland, though all countries, the latter two in particular, have produced a number of films and television series set prior to the events of 1989.

Additionally, the character Dr Zeiske (played by Winfried Glatzeder, who is famous for his portrayal of Paul in *Die Legende von Paul und Paula*) travels back from New York and brings gifts to his colleagues. The items provoke much hilarity as they exchange knowing jokes about his surviving the evils of capitalism. Schmith enters and quips to Zeiske 'Hello, globe trotter – how is imperialism?' 'As pre-ordained, it's decaying,' jokes Zeiske in reply. He then expands on the theme to colleagues, saying: 'despite Berlin's filth, it's a sterile operation room compared to New York'. Whilst this could be interpreted as a propagandistic swipe at 'the imperialists' to a contemporary viewer, one only need view any New York-shot film from the late 1970s to have as much confirmed from an outside source. The opposite of this scene is frequently played out in Western depictions of the GDR, but in these lighthearted depictions of the chasm between the official state position and the more relaxed personal understanding of the bland reality of the Cold War as lived by people, it is not to be found. From the outset, then, Roland Gräf's film defies the reductive tropes we have been taught to associate with the GDR.

The film's protagonist, Dr Schmith (Armin Müller-Stahl), is a successful medical professional who due to the continued rejection of his research proposals feels his important research into premature infant mortality rates will be better funded in West Germany. The film clearly implies that he too will be more handsomely funded on a personal level, Schmith's superior Frau Professor Mettenzwei stating that 'we all know that West doctors earn five to ten times more'. Schmith is also clearly non-political and is identified as such several times in the film. This can be both an advantage, as when a colleague jovially states 'we non-party members must stick together', and a disadvantage. His superiors, Professor Mettenzwei and Professor Meissner, both implore him to take a more active political role and suggest it would augment the support of his research. On each occasion, Schmith demurs. This reluctance to work with others or join in is central to Schmith's dilemma and forms the central arc of the plot. His problem is indecision, which is a result of his selfish character, and will eventually bring about his downfall.

An early scene with a colleague foreshadows this. Gudrun, revealed to be a former lover, surprises Schmith by smoking. When he asks 'why didn't I know you smoked?', she replies 'because you're so preoccupied with yourself'. She reveals that she is getting married to a man she doesn't love, as she did Schmith, but that he is 'the first person in the evening to ask me how I got through the day. Do you understand? He asks *me*.' Schmith, sentimental and aroused by his former lover, is too focused on a farewell bout of intimacy to heed her last remark when Gudrun says 'I thought that might be a tip for you.' Not asking is something he will later pay dearly for.

At the beginning of the film, Schmith meets with a people smuggler, Lenkert, at an autobahn restaurant near the border. Lenkert gives him his documents and confirms that he has been accepted as head doctor in a child's clinic in Inntal, West Germany. 'I'll accept your offer,' he confirms, though he will undermine this assertive beginning henceforth. The tension of this assertion is underscored by a group of students at an adjacent table who suggest a conflicting direction of movement when they sing a bouyant vacation anthem carrying the refrain 'we're off to the Soviet Union'. They might be, but not Schmith it seems. His central conflict emerges almost immediately afterwards when he visits his father to tell of his planned departure west. 'No one will rain on my parade again,' declares Schmith. 'Someone will always rain on your parade, here (East) as there (West),' retorts his father. As he tries to convince his father to follow him west, his selfish streak first emerges. He wants those around him to bend to his will, to follow him; he does not 'want to be smothered in this pettiness'.

In *Die Flucht*, the character of Schmith strides the border between East and West. Non-political, he is unconcerned with the workings of the state, but financial gain is not what motivates him. Schmith's colleague Wendt draws Professor Mettenzwei's opprobrium and scorn when he tries to flee over the Austrian–Hungarian border. 'To me, anyone who leaves, likeable or not, is a traitor.' Welcomed back to the hospital and his job, Wendt cuts a forlorn figure, resented by colleagues for his disloyalty. Significantly, Schmith too shows contempt for him, even though he is currently planning a similar venture. When Schmith and Wendt discuss the matter, Wendt confirms that his wife's inheritance in the West was his reason for attempting to flee but implores Schmith to believe that he 'remains loyal to our government and socialist state'. Schmith coldly asks 'don't you see how pitiful you're acting?' and walks out.

Schmith's plans to leave for the West begin to change when he falls in love with a young doctor who joins his clinic. As his romance with Katharina (Jenny Gröllmann) evolves, his work prospects find a sudden change of fortune. A Czechoslovakian medical institution offer to co-fund his research for a larger amount than he had initially sought. This means he can achieve his goals in the GDR and stay in the relationship with Katharina. The subsequent choice he makes to remain in the GDR is where the thriller plot gains its tautness. Previously, the tension of the moral dilemma at the heart of the film – to flee or not to flee – transforms on a more practical dimension when Schmith makes a trip to Cologne. He visits the hospital that bid for his expertise but also encounters the smuggler whom he let down by not sticking to the arranged plan. He is now under pressure to keep the arrangement, so his situation has been reversed. Instead of seeking to flee to develop his research, he now must abandon his lover to fulfil his obligation. After a menacing visit by a man to his clinic back in East Germany, Schmith knows he is being watched by the smugglers and that his professional life is at risk. It is this dilemma that gives the film its edge.

Schmith cannot go to the police as his career will be over due to his plans to flee, thus the film acknowledges the repressive position of the state with regard to defectors. Schmith does not want to become Wendt, whom he holds in disdain, but wants to free himself of his criminal obligations whilst soaring career-wise.

His selfishness and indecision have brought this upon him. Had he been patient, he would have got his research funding and been able to retain his relationship with Katharina, but his selfishness caused him to seek departure. Had he been decisive, he would have already left. At one point, he broods whilst walking with Katharina that he feels 'like Buridan's donkey' who 'starves between two stacks of hay'. At this point unaware of his dilemma between East or West, she states that she 'only sees one stack, and it's very big'.

Ultimately, with pressure mounting, he chooses to go west with Katharina but neglects to tell her of his plan, failing to heed Gudrun's tip from earlier. After spending a weekend in a dacha, ostensibly for a short break, he wakes Katharina early to leave and only informs her of his plan to go west moments before he is to meet the smugglers. Katharina flees, feeling she does not have sufficient time to make the choice, and Schmith, having already shown he is unreliable, gets into a fight with the smugglers, who strike him over the head and leave him unconscious on the autobahn. The blow causes an unspecified ailment that Schmith has been concealing to prompt a seizure that kills him. The closing shot of the film shows the deserted slipway where he died, empty of any trace of him, as cars drive in westerly and easterly directions on the autobahn behind. The shot becomes a metaphor for Schmith's indecision and how by procrastinating as to which direction he should take, he ends up forever alone, travelling nowhere on the slipway.

Katharina's fleeing (back to the GDR) sets up a compelling dynamic. It is not that she fears a life in the West but she rather feels betrayed because Schmith did not inform her of his plans. (Again, Gudrun's tip is pertinent: 'He asks *me*.') Lives are complicated, with emotional ties to family and friends, and Schmith has forced Katharina to choose a life with him at his behest. Overwhelmed, she asserts her autonomy and right to choose by running into the woods. Noticeably, this is in direct contrast to films such as *Barbara* and *Das Leben der Anderen*: in the former, Barbara forgoes the opportunity to flee west to allow a young former patient, Stella, to go in her stead. In so doing, she gives up her lover in the West and accepts a life with the sympathetic Stasi doctor André. In the latter, Christa-Maria first sleeps with her Stasi handler Hempf to protect her partner Dreyman, whom she then betrays through interrogation anyway, and finding no way out, she kills herself. In both films, women are depicted as having to submit to the Stasi – represented through male authority – to find a way to express their freedom of choice. In *Die Flucht*, Katharina asserts the ability to choose by not relenting to male authority in the form of Schmith's demand that she leave with him. It is noteworthy that a film produced within the GDR depicts a woman with greater agency than a film set in the GDR made after the fact. The character of Lenkert is of similar note: a character who resides in the West though can travel freely east, he exploits those who lack his freedom of movement. When Schmith's romantic involvement with Katharina compromises Lenkert's plans, and by extension his connections, he forces Schmith to follow through on his agreement, irrespective of the emotional and personal cost, which for Schmith turns out to be the ultimate cost.

The period of creative freedom in East German cinema would last until around 1985, with film attendance being at between seventy million and eighty million per year through the decade. *Platoon* (Oliver Stone, 1986), *Dirty Dancing* (Emile Ardolino, 1987) and *The Name of the Rose* (Jean-Jacques Annaud, 1986) were all successful at the East German box office, showing that 'unavoidable vice' was still drawing in audiences. But as Honecker pulled against Gorbachev's *glasnost*, the last four years of the GDR saw a reduction in the number of Western films released, with two thirds of those distributed in 1987 coming from socialist countries. And, whilst films lauding the merits of the Stalinist gerontocracy did not permeate, neither did films that challenged the status quo. The last film released in the GDR was Heiner Carow's *Coming Out*, which had its premiere in the Kino International on Karl-Marx-Allee on 9 November 1989, the same night Günther Schabowski, an official of the Socialist Unity Party, went on television for a press conference in which, when asked about the relaxing of inter-German border controls, he uttered the words '*Das tritt nach meiner Kenntnis ... ist das sofort ... unverzüglich*' ('As far as I know ... effective immediate, without delay'), in effect ushering in free movement.

Carow's film got lost in what followed, but it was another film that sought to challenge thematic taboos as it looked at the repression of homosexuality in East German society. After 1989, film attendance figures dropped to as low as twelve million per annum, and as DEFA was privatised, studio staff complained that whilst previously they had been restricted by ideological censorship, now they were restricted by economic censorship.

Some historical notes are worth pointing out with regard to *Die Flucht*. The film was lead actor Armin Müller-Stahl's last DEFA film. Müller-Stahl had requested to emigrate to West Germany prior to filming, but after criticising East German protest musician Wolf Biermann being stripped of his GDR citizenship whilst touring in West Germany, Müller-Stahl was subsequently blacklisted. His next film appearance would be in Fassbinder's *Lola* (1981). Müller-Stahl's co-star Jenny Gröllmann remained an actor in the GDR and went on to marry fellow actor Ulrich Mühe, who played the leading role of the Stasi agent Wiesler in *Das Leben der Anderen*. When Mühe gained access to his Stasi file after the fall of communism, he discovered that Gröllmann was recorded as having informed on him. Gröllmann denied the accusation and won an injunction against Mühe, preventing him from publishing an account of his beliefs in his autobiography.

A final irony that strikes me is the fact that I am writing from the same building that the historian Timothy Garton Ash lived in for nine months in 1980 whilst under supervision by the Stasi, an experience he wrote about memorably in his 1997 book *The File*. His personal file recounts the observations informer 'Schuldt' made whilst searching his room in his absence:

> The door to the room is closed from inside with a security lock that appears to have been fitted only recently. Apart from a bed, a table and a pair of chairs, one notices above all a large sideboard on which the tenant has – as I discovered – mainly put books. Newspapers were laid out on the table (I noticed, above all, several copies of *Sonntag*) on which marginalia bore witness to intense reading.
>
> 1997: 66–67

Whilst the GDR was certainly lacking in democracy and individual freedom, as the above quote demonstrates, there were opportunities to make compelling, nuanced and dynamic artistic gestures within the vagaries of a restricted system such as that presided over by a figure such as Erich Honecker. These gestures, *Die Flucht* being an exemplary case, are done a great disservice when swept away with the justifiable criticisms of the society within which they were produced. Through a closer reading and appreciation of films such as Gräf's, a broader and more nuanced understanding of the political climate both within and beyond the borders of the former state can be discerned.

References

Allan, S. and Sandford, J. (1999). *DEFA – East German Cinema, 1946–1992*. Oxford: Berghahn Books.
Fulbrook, M. (2005). *The People's State*. New Haven: Yale University Press.
Garton Ash, T. (1997). *The File: A Personal History*. New York: Vintage.
Kalb, M. (2020). *Coming of Age: Constructing and Controlling Youth in Munich, 1942–1973*. Oxford: Berghahn Books.

15

Days of '36 (Meres tou '36), Theo Angelopoulos, 1972

Eleftheria Rania Kosmidou

Figure 16 *Days of '36* (1972), courtesy of Artificial Eye

When asked to introduce *Days of '36* as part of the *States of Danger and Deceit* season at HOME, I thought to myself, what can I say about Theo Angelopoulos and the film in just a few minutes? I have written about his films and I have written about the ways in which his films affect Brechtian aesthetics (Kosmidou, 2017). I have gone against the grain and argued that his films cannot be considered textbook Brechtian despite being considered by many as such (Horton, 1997; Jordan, 2000; Karalis, 2006; Rollet, 2012). It is precisely his ability to affect and alter Brechtian aesthetics that makes him one of the best and most important contemporary filmmakers, a master of cinematic style and a master of allegory, a modernist, a 'poet of images' (Mania, 2012), an *auteur* indeed.

His films, shot on location, are usually set on the cold, misty and often rainy background of Northern Greece. There are myriad accounts of how Angelopoulos used to travel in the north of Greece, through and around villages and small towns, trying to find places where he could set his films, waiting for days at times for the right weather, namely, winter-looking conditions, to set his films in and start shooting (conditions not so sparse in the winter in Greece but an almost impossible task in summertime).

Elaborate *mise en scène* and distinct camera movement are his signature style. His cinema is melancholic and meditative, a cinema in which the camera interprets the events shown. His work has won awards at many film festivals around the world and has been compared to the works of Jancso, and Straub and Huillet, filmmakers who rejected realistic representations of history in favour of a Brechtian approach to cinema and allegorical representations of history on screen. His style has been compared to Tarkovsky's and, at times, to Antonioni's. However, his films are political above everything else. His films are about Greek history, myth and memory, about the impact of Greek history – one of wars, occupations, dictatorships, immigration, borders and alienation – on the present. To paraphrase the Greek critic Vassilis Rafailidis (2018), the fog in Angelopoulos's films is not a meteorological phenomenon; it is a historical one.

Angelopoulos shows representations of historical events to talk about the present. In this way, his films are political allegories of a past that is still present, and in doing so, in a Brechtian way, he demands an active viewing from his audience. He makes use of the Brechtian defamiliarisation effects (V-effects) – episodic narratives, characters not presented psychologically to the audience, stylised acting, the use of songs to interpret the narrative, gestus – in his films to make the audience think. In contrast to Brechtian aesthetics, however, the past in his films affects his characters in a teleological way as they are always invested with disillusionment, a lack of desire and, ultimately, and importantly in contrast to Brechtian aesthetics, a lack of hope. They are always the victims of a past they cannot escape from.

Theo Angelopoulos was raised in Athens. He started studying law at the University of Athens but never finished his degree; he moved to Paris instead to study film. He worked for the ethnographic filmmaker Jean Rouch for a while, and when he returned back to Greece in 1963, he worked for the left-wing journal *Demokratiki Allaggi* as a film critic, before he made his first feature film *Reconstruction (Anaparastasi)* in 1970, a film based on the real-life murder of a Greek worker in Germany by his wife and her lover. In this film, the reconstruction of the murder becomes an allegory for the disruption of life in Greece under the military regime (the Colonels' regime) at the time.

Days of '36 is the second feature film made by Angelopoulos. It is the first film in his so-called history films, but I would say it is the first of his most overtly political films as well, the second being *The Travelling Players (O thiasos)* made in 1975, followed by *The Hunters (Oi kynigoi)* in 1977 and finally *Alexander the Great (O Megalexandros)* in 1980. *Days of '36* and *The Travelling Players* were made during the Colonels' dictatorship in Greece, namely, the Junta (1967–1974), whilst *The Travelling Players* was finished a year after the fall of the Colonels' regime. *Days of '36* is set in 1936 at the end of the Second Republic (which had abolished the monarchy in Greece) and just before the royalist dictatorship of General Ioannis Metaxas (1936–1941), or the '4th of August' regime as it is called, was established. The increasing pressure and the lingering fascism of the Metaxas government that came to power in 1936, as well as murders and conspiracies, are hinted at throughout *Days of '36*, a film that deals with a specific time in Greek history of course. The film is a study of political power. Angelopoulos's study of political power in his work, however, is not a general one but specific: it is the power of the Greek right that he explores in his films. The film was photographed by George Arvanitis, a cinematographer with whom Angelopoulos worked until the 1990s. It won the Best Director and Best Cinematography awards at the Thessaloniki Film Festival in 1972, as well as the *Fipresci* (the critics') award at the Berlin Film Festival Forum in 1973.

What is lingering in *Days of '36* is the subject matter of his next two films, *The Travelling Players* (1975) and *The Hunters* (1977). The former follows an acting troupe around Greece, from General Metaxas's dictatorship in 1936 through World War II, the Greek

Civil War and the Cold War up to the election of Greek Marshal Alexandros Papagos in 1952. As the troupe travels, history affects and transforms its members. The film was shot under the Colonels' regime, and to avoid the censors, Angelopoulos used two main dramatic intertexts as structuring devices, namely, the myth of the Atrides and the melodramatic folk play *Golpho*. Throughout the film, the troupe attempts to perform *Golpho*, written by Spyros Peresiadis in 1893, but each performance is interrupted, and every interruption of the play is caused by very specific historical and political circumstances, such as the Italian invasion of Greece in 1940. *The Hunters* is set in 1977. On New Year's Eve, six bourgeois hunters find a dead body in the snow, the body of a left-wing guerilla fighter killed during the Greek Civil War. The body is preserved and still bleeding, despite the fact that the Civil War ended in 1949. They take the body inside the hotel they are staying in with their wives and place it on a table in the lobby. Each member of the group then speaks of his experiences of the Civil War as they give their statements to the police officer. *The Hunters*, as Fredric Jameson stated (2012: 68), is 'an extraordinary allegory for the persistence of guilt' of the winners of the Greek Civil War, namely, the Greek right. In *Alexander the Great*, the filmmaker juxtaposes the ancient history of Greece with the present. In the film, Alexander is a former political prisoner (left wing) who kidnaps British tourists for ransom until Britain and the puppet government in Athens meet his demands for amnesty for his group, the freedom fighters. The film asks the audience to view Greek ancient history not as a noble past but as the remnants of an ongoing pillage.

After the above historical films, Angelopoulos made his so-called 'Trilogy of Silence': the silence of history, *Voyage to Cythera* (*Taxidi sta Kythira*, 1983); the silence of love, *The Beekeeper* (*O melissokomos*, 1986); and the silence of God, *Landscape in the Mist* (*Topio stin omihli*, 1988) – three films which explore the odysseys, disillusionment and alienation of their characters and their personal journeys, coming-of-age stories as well as spiritual enlightenment stories. They are also, however, historical and political allegories of Greece's emergence from years of dictatorships and wars. *The Suspended Step of the Stork* (*To meteoro vima tou pelargou*, 1991), *Ulysses's Gaze* (*To vlemma tou Odyssea*, 1995) and *Eternity and a Day* (*Mia aioniotita kai mia mera*, 1998) mark his 'trilogy of borders', with an interest in borders and boundaries in the Balkans. Characters are stuck in between their borders, with boundaries blurred under the mist, rain and snow. These three films deal with the concept of the 'border' as an abstract notion, whilst they represent, we could argue, a denunciation of the border as a whole. As Mastroianni asks in *The Suspended Step of the Stork*, 'We've crossed the border and we're still here ... How many borders must we cross to reach home? Where is home, the place we are at peace?' These films are also about history and thus deeply political, as they deal with Greece and the Balkans.

Angelopoulos's last films were part of an incomplete trilogy of Greek history: *The Weeping Meadow* (*Trilogia: To livadi pou dakryzei*) made in 2004, which spans events from 1919 to the aftermath of World War II as it tells Greek history through the sufferings of one family; *The Dust of Time* (*Trilogia II: I skoni tou hronou*) in 2008, which spans the traumas of the period after the end of World War II until the end of the twentieth century; whilst the last of the trilogy, *The Other Sea*, set in the present (2012), was left incomplete due to the filmmaker's sudden death in a motorcycle accident on the set one night in 2012 at the age of seventy-six.

Days of '36 is arguably a film about how the Metaxas dictatorship was established. In the film, a few months before Metaxas came to power in 1936, a unionist is murdered in a crowded square in broad daylight. The suspect, Sofianos, a left-wing, ex-police collaborator, currently a political prisoner, tries to prove his innocence in vain. The political powers do not believe him. When a friend of his, an MP, visits him in his cell, he takes him hostage and threatens to kill him if he is not set free. A few months before the 1936 elections, the Metaxas government is thus in a difficult position: if they resist Sofianos's blackmail and the MP is murdered, they will lose the support from the Greek right, which they need; if they let Sofianos free, they will lose the support from the Greek centre, which they also need. What prevailed in the end is clearly shown in the closing scene of the film with the execution of the demonstrators.

The film opens and closes with a murder. In the opening scene, in bird's-eye view shots of a square, we observe demonstrators gathering. The camera in medium shots follows a man walking through the crowd as he gets on stage to deliver his speech. Suddenly, he is shot dead and the gathered demonstrators start running away whilst the camera stays still on the dead body on the ground and it then zooms out to an extreme long shot to show us a man attending to the body. After Sofianos is shot dead in his cell, the film ends with a scene in which soldiers of the Metaxas government execute the demonstrators lined up in a field. The film thus starts and ends with murders pointing to the political conditions of the time just before the Metaxas government was established and their growing authoritarianism. However, filmed during another dictatorship, as mentioned above, the film is also an allegory of the intrigues and increasing authoritarianism of the Colonels' regime that was established in 1967.

The opening scenes of *Days of '36* are emblematic of the filmmaker's style and cinematic techniques (techniques which he perfected in his next film, *The Travelling Players*): characters are not presented psychologically to us; violence is implied or 'shown' off screen; shots are empty of figures in long takes and plan sequences; songs are used in a diegetic way as they interpret the events shown; there are long shots and bird's-eye view shots (reminiscent perhaps of Angelopoulos's work with Rouch and the cinema vérité tradition); and a camera that most of the time is static until it is not and pans to the left or right to find the action, at times in a circular, 360-degree pan – all reoccurring stylistic choices in his work. We, the audience, observe the events shown and are being asked to contemplate them, whilst at no point any straightforward answers are given.

We never see what happens in Sofianos's cell, for example. In fact, the important political events, and most of the action in the film, take place behind doors, behind walls, doorways or windows, whilst bird's-eye view shots of a staircase and of the prison make the prison look impossible to escape from. Often, we cannot see the characters' faces or even hear what they are saying. We cannot hear any important political conversations and decisions; they are always filmed in extreme long shots whilst the few conversations we can hear are not in-depth and crucial to the events of the story. Everything is implied; crucially, everything is almost faceless. In this way, Angelopoulos and Arvanitis highlight the fact that the protagonists of the story can be anybody. Politics and history are taking place in secrecy, in the shadows. And we, the audience, are kept in the dark. The camerawork interprets and encodes the events of the film as it shows events that are not meant to be shown at the time the film was made, events that were forbidden to be discussed. After all, as the filmmaker said, the film:

> was shot during the dictatorship. What is important in the film, I tried to place it behind doors, to be discussed behind doors, or on the phone, so it is not directly discussed or whispered. The dictatorship is the form of the film. These were the conditions under which I was working: I could not speak.
>
> Ciment and Tierchant, 1989: 52

Silences prevail in the film, and silences say more here. In this way, not only does the filmmaker manage to avoid the censors, he also manages to distance the audience in a Brechtian way and make them think. At the same time, questions are left unanswered. Who killed the unionist? What was Sofianos's role? Why did the MP get involved? As we, the distanced audience, watch the film, we become more and more suspicious of the political powers of the time. Meanwhile, the events presented in the film suspiciously resemble real events that took place in 1936, as Nikos Skoplakis rightly points out (2017): the extreme right-wing party member Marinos who was imprisoned for murder but under privileged conditions, as he was the lover of a conservative MP; the smuggling of a gun inside the prison; Marinos taking the MP and his lover as hostages; and the Metaxas government justifying their growing authoritarianism. The film, made during another dictatorship, is an allegory of the continuation of the past into the present, an allegory of a cycle of dictatorships and suffering in Greece since 1936. In an interview with David Jenkins in *Sight and Sound*, Angelopoulos said:

> Days of '36 refers to the Metaxa dictatorship of 1936 and was filmed during the dictatorship of the 1970s. It was with this film that I had to change the way I spoke as a filmmaker. Everything became suggested or implied. When Days of '36 was first shown in Athens, there were people in the audience who started asking questions. I was surprised when I realised that those people weren't the police. I remember one woman handed me some flowers and asked: had she really understood everything she had just seen? And of course I said yes. In the spirit of the film, even this dialogue with the audience was suggested and implied.
>
> 2012

Days of '36 is different from Angelopoulos's other films and I am not the only one to note this. Vasiliou (2013) states that *Days of '36* is full of bright lights, when he claims that 'never again, neither the sun, nor the lively lights that remind us of watercolours, will have such an important presence in his films'.[1] The narrative of the film is linear, yet there is no obvious protagonist/hero which affects the narrative dynamically, as is usually the case. The camerawork at times seems indifferent to the events of the film, as Angelopoulos and Arvanitis film the important events in tracking shots and bird's-eye view shots. The camera always seems to be in the wrong position trying to find the action. But as I mentioned above, there is no action; the action happens off screen. It is as if nothing happens in the film. It is a film in which Hollywood's cause-and-effect trope is totally absent. As Vasiliou (2013) describes, 'from the 104 minutes of the film, we have to wait more than 30 minutes to hear the first complete sentence which informs us about the important elements of the story: that the manager of the prison informs the military and judicial leadership on Sofianos's profile and Kriezi's hostage-taking'. In this way, the narrative gaps become the protagonists of the film indeed.

Note

1 'Ποτέ ξανά, ούτε ο ήλιος, ούτε τα ζωντανά χρώματα που θυμίζουν ακουαρέλα, δε θα έχουν τόσο σημαντική παρουσία σε άλλη του ταινία' (my translation).

References

Ciment, M. and Tierchant, H. (1989). *Théo Angelopoulos*. Paris: Edilig.
Horton, A. (1997). *The Films of Theo Angelopoulos: A Cinema of Contemplation*. Princeton, NJ: Princeton University Press.
Jameson, F. (2012). 'The Past as History, the Future as Form'. In E. Stathi (Ed.), *Theo Angelopoulos*. Thessaloniki: Thessaloniki Film Festival Publications, 65–86.
Jenkins, D. (2012). 'The Sweep of History'. *Sight and Sound*, 22(2), 52–55.
Jordan, I. (2000). 'For an Epic Theatre'. In E. Stathi (Ed.), *Theo Angelopoulos*. Athens: Kastaniotis, 232–240.

Karalis, V. (2006). 'The Disjunctive Aesthetics of Myth and Empathy in Theo Angelopoulos' Ulysses Gaze'. *Literature and Aesthetics*, 16(2), 252–268.

Kosmidou, E. (2017). 'Theo Angelopoulos's *O Thiasos/The Travelling Players* (1975) and *Oi Kynigoi/The Hunters* (1977) and How They Affect the Brechtian Project'. *Journal of Modern Greek Studies*, 35, 513–538.

Mania, P. (2012). 'For Theo Angelopoulos'. Retrieved from: www.photolo gio.gr/fotografia-stin-7i-texni/theo-angelopoulos/

Rafailidis, V. (2018, 24 January). 'The Foggy Greek History in Angelopoulos's Films'. *Katiousa*. Retrieved from: www.katiousa.gr/pol itismos/kinimatografos/v-rafailidis-omichlodis-elliniki-istoria-stis-tain ies-tou-angelopoulou/

Rollet, S. (2012). 'Theatre versus Image'. In E. Stathi (Ed.), *Theo Angelopoulos*. Athens: Thessaloniki Film Festival Publications, 54–61.

Skoplakis, N. (2017). 'For *Days of '36* – To Theo Angelopoulos's Memory'. Retrieved from: www.osxoliastis.gr/

Vasiliou, T. (2013, 14 September). 'Theo Angelopoulos's *Days of '36*: History as Cinematic Form'. Retrieved from: https://barikat.gr/cont ent/meres-toy-36-toy-thodoroy-aggelopoyloy-i-istoria-os-kinimatograf iki-forma

16

Who is the man on the roof?

Roy Stafford

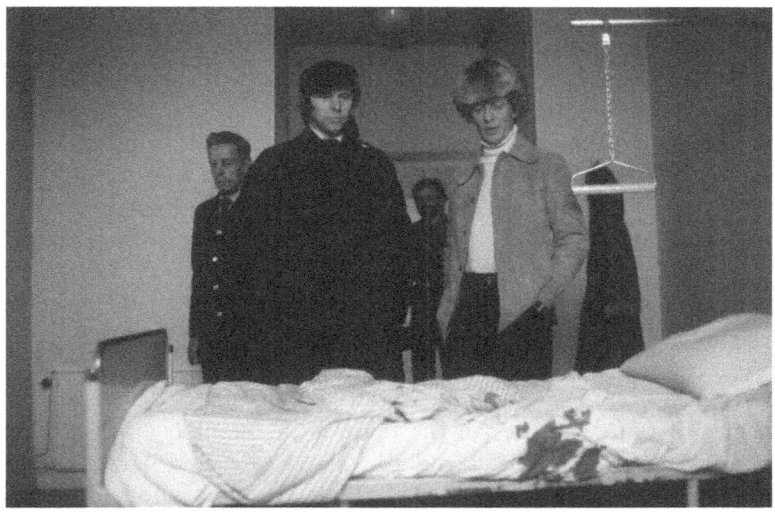

Figure 17 Advertising poster for *Man on the Roof* (1976), courtesy of Svenska Film Institut

If we were compiling a film season of 'European political thrillers' from the twenty-first century, we might immediately think of something dark that dealt with threats against social democracy. An adaptation of one of Stieg Larsson's *Millennium Trilogy* of novels might fit the bill. These dealt with violence against women, incipient fascism and corruption in the Swedish intelligence services. For many audiences around the world, these books and films introduced the concept of 'Nordic Noir' alongside distinctive TV serials such as

Forbrydelsen (*The Killing*, Denmark–Norway–Sweden–Germany, 2007–2012) and *Bron/Broen* (*The Bridge*, Sweden–Denmark–Germany, 2011–2018). But what of the 1970s in Scandinavia? Could we find the same political thrillers then? Some 1970s audiences in the UK might have known the name Ingmar Bergman, almost synonymous with the idea of a dark and twisted Swedish art film. But Bergman did not make films with many thrills or with much concern about contemporary politics. However, there is a direct link during the 1970s to the modern idea of Nordic Noir and it concerns a pair of Swedish writers who conceived a new kind of police hero in the 1960s, one who would become the character who did not just catch the bad guys but went about the job in a way that exposed political problems. And this character, a 'revolutionary' in terms of crime fiction, would not only survive and thrive in his contemporary world of crime fiction but would also act as a direct inspiration for many of the writers and filmmakers who produced works of Nordic Noir from 1990 onwards. This chapter explores the film adaptation of one of the novels featuring this 'political detective', Martin Beck.

Maj Sjöwall and Per Wahlöö: the story of a crime

Maj Sjöwall and Per Wahlöö were two committed socialists who began to write together in the mid-1960s. Wahlöö (1926–1975) had been a crime reporter and all-round writer and had travelled widely. He was older than Sjöwall (born in 1935), who had been a rebellious young woman (with a small child) but was employed as a magazine journalist and art director when she met Wahlöö as a colleague working on other magazines for the same publisher. They had what would then have been considered a 'modern' relationship, never marrying but having two children together and writing their books in the evenings when the kids were in bed.

The couple shared the same sense of a collapsing Swedish welfare state which had developed in the late 1930s but by the 1960s was, in their view, failing the working class badly. They decided, in Wahlöö's words, to 'use the crime novel as a scalpel cutting open the belly of the ideological, pauperised and morally debatable so-called welfare state' (Liukkonen, 2008). What was so revolutionary about their project was perhaps not their political stance but their formal idea. They effectively invented what is now described as the modern 'long-form narrative', devoured today by audiences in the form of 'box-sets' of TV serials, planning ten crime fiction novels featuring the same police detectives. The novels were to be written roughly one a year between 1965 and 1975. The last was completed with Wahlöö seriously ill and he died before it was published. The ten-novel serial had a subtitle – *The Story of a Crime* – which critics have interpreted as referring to the nationalisation of the Swedish police force in 1965 and the decline in its effectiveness because of poor management and central control. During this period, it also became more of a paramilitary force with greater firepower and less interest in protecting the community.

The ten books developed a serial form as although each book focused on one or possibly two linked crime investigations, the focus on the two central detectives and their domestic lives formed a continuous narrative. The books have remained in print since their first publication and current editions are each introduced by a popular contemporary crime author such as Henning Mankell, Val McDermid and Arne Dahl. Lee Child's introduction to the book, adapted as the film *The Man on the Roof* in 1976, the main work discussed in this chapter, starts like this:

> Nations are stereotyped as easily as anything else, and in the 1960s and 70s most of us thought of Sweden as a paradise, where social democracy worked, where the welfare state was successful, where the girls were blonde and beautiful, where the scenery was lovely and the buildings half-timbered, and where sexuality was frank and innocent. Maj Sjöwall and Per Wahlöö lived there, and knew different.
>
> In Sjöwall and Wahlöö, 2016: 8

The long writing process meant that the nature of the crimes and the investigations developed over time. The first three novels, *Roseanna* (1965), *The Man Who Went up in Smoke* (1966) and *The Man on the Balcony* (1967), grappled with the idea of introducing a new kind of Swedish crime fiction opposed to the traditional Swedish crime novels which followed the classic British format exemplified by Agatha Christie. Sjöwall and Wahlöö wanted to bring more realism into their settings and to focus on a team of police officers and the procedures they followed in attempting to solve crimes.

They dealt with crimes that had either happened somewhere in the world or were plausible in the settings they described. *Roseanna* was inspired by a canal trip by the authors during which they spotted a tourist: 'There was an American woman on the boat, beautiful, with dark hair, always standing alone. I caught Per looking at her. "Why don't we start the book by killing this woman?"' Sjöwall suggested (in Liukkonen, 2008). This led to painstaking work on the stages of the subsequent police investigation. Their realistic crimes often took several weeks or even months for the detectives to solve.

The police procedural crime fiction novel had already been established by Georges Simenon with Inspector Maigret (1931–1972) and Ed McBain in his *87th Precinct* novels (1956–2005) but not with the same political subtext. The first few novels of *The Story of a Crime* (or the 'Project' as Sjöwall described it) developed the approach, the writing style and the characters, but the strong political viewpoint did not become so pronounced until around Book 5. Each book involves the same group of 'Criminal Police' (something like the CID in the UK) operating out of Stockholm but sometimes deployed nationally and on one occasion internationally. The central character is Martin Beck, initially an Inspector and then gradually promoted, though he refuses the top jobs. Beck is characterised as that now familiar figure, the police detective with the unsatisfactory marriage but a clear sense of where he stands on the dangers to social democracy.

The team of detectives changes over time but five names emerge. They are not glamorous types and are not sociable. Beck has only Lennart Kollberg as his friend. Kollberg is an ex-paratrooper who refuses to carry a weapon and whilst happy with his wife and child is increasingly angry with the police as an institution. Gunwald Larsson, an aggressive and headstrong member of the team, becomes an important character in the second half of the serial. The other two significant team members are Rönn, a dogged investigator from northern Sweden, and Melander, whose function is to act like a human database of past cases in a period before computers became available.

Beck might be 'revolutionary' in terms of the conventions of detective fiction but he is not a heroic figure. He gets car sick and travels by train and taxi. At the end of Book 9, Kollberg resigns. He is the socialist who cannot cope with the work any more. The final book leads to the death of the Swedish Prime Minister in a shooting.

In 1986, the Swedish premier Olaf Palme was assassinated, a terrible event which the Beck novels seemed to have predicted. The death of Palme as a major political/social event was very important for the crime writer Henning Mankell, whose first Inspector Wallander book appeared in 1991. Mankell shared the same political viewpoint as Sjöwall and Wahlöö and his detective is clearly related to Martin Beck. It is through Wallander – the novels and TV series – that a new generation in the UK rediscovered the Beck books that inspired Mankell.

Adapting the Beck novels

The ten Martin Beck novels have all been adapted for film and/or TV. The novels themselves were not at first massively popular in Sweden and, to some extent, it was the international response that encouraged the two authors. The adaptations reflected this international interest. The first three adaptations included a Hollywood film adaptation of *The Laughing Policeman* (Book 4, 1968), directed by Stuart Rosenberg and starring Walter Matthau as Beck. Critics saw this film as removing much of the political subtext. Other adaptations appeared in the USSR, Germany and the Netherlands. In the 1990s, six Swedish TV film adaptations appeared (the line between films for TV and films for cinema is much less defined in Sweden). Two of them were directed by Daniel Alfredson, who would later direct Parts 2 and 3 of the *Millennium* adaptations. Gunwald Larsson is played by Rolf Lassgård in all six films. Lassgård became the first TV/film incarnation of Kurt Wallander in roughly the same period. The latest TV series, titled *Beck*, produced fifty-two episodes between 1997 and 2023 with Peter Haber as Martin, now taking a back seat on new stories featuring a younger team. Gunwald Larsson (Mikael Persbrandt) was included up to 2016.

Book 7, *The Abominable Man*, was adapted in 1976 as *The Man on the Roof*, with the screenplay and direction by Bo Widerberg. Widerberg (1930–1997) was the best possible adapter of a Beck novel. He had a similar political stance to the authors and the same ideas for presenting the story. In the 1960s and early 1970s, he was arguably one of the two most important Swedish film directors. Significantly, he was opposed to the dominant figure of Ingmar Bergman.

Like Sjöwall, Widerberg was a rebellious youth, leaving school at seventeen, deserting from army service, writing prolifically – novels and short stories – then becoming a film critic and making his first feature in 1962. He was only twelve years younger than Bergman, but because Bergman started earlier as a scriptwriter and theatre director in his mid-twenties, the two men seemed to come from different generations. Widerberg saw Bergman as representing conservative, high-culture Sweden, drawing on theatre and the tradition of Swedish craftmanship and thus ignoring aesthetic developments elsewhere in the world. Widerberg grew up in a working-class but artistically inclined family in Malmö. He had travelled to overseas festivals and absorbed ideas about how to represent more realistic images of Sweden and ordinary Swedes.

In 1962, Widerberg published *Visionen i svensk film* (*A Vision of Swedish Cinema*), in which he accused Swedish film of being insular and mummified. When he began to direct, he chose story scenarios drawing on his knowledge of Malmö in the 1930s and 1940s, which he presented in a style drawing on neorealism and the French New Wave. The semi-autobiographical *Raven's End* (1963) was the first of five of his films in competition for the *Palme d'Or* at the Cannes Film Festival. Two of them, *Ådalen 31* (1969), about a confrontation between striking workers and the military, and *Joe Hill* (1971), about the Swedish-American labour activist, won Jury prizes. A third film from this period, *Elvira Madigan* (1967), was one of the major box office successes around Europe in 1967/1968. This story of the doomed nineteenth-century romance between a teenage Danish ballet dancer and a young aristocratic Swedish military officer was in part a commentary on the social attitudes of the period. It was also innovatory in its use of natural light for a summer romance in colour accompanied by Mozart and Vivaldi. These last three titles confirmed Widerberg's status as a major director, not just in Sweden but internationally.

The Abominable Man

When he came to adapt *The Abominable Man*, Widerberg put virtually the whole narrative, including much of the original dialogue, on screen more or less exactly as written. For a film of 107 minutes, he had to find ways of representing some dialogue and description visually. *The Man on the Roof* was filmed on location in Stockholm and it is one of the most 'realist' crime films ever made. The five detectives are in one sense 'ordinary'. Their police work is routine procedure and sometimes clumsy in execution. As a line in the novel states, 'Police work is built on realism, routine, stubbornness and system' (Maj Sjöwall and Per Wahlöö, 2016: 48). Widerberg showed imagination in casting Carl-Gustaf Lindstedt as Beck. Lindstedt was a comedian and comic actor and this was one of his first dramatic roles. His father was a Social Democrat politician and Lindstedt had learned his trade in socialist youth theatre. His tired look and careful plain-speaking are crucial elements in his creation of the central character. His Beck does not always make the right decisions and he personally doesn't have strong political views. It is important in the story that Beck and Rönn have to work without sleep in this narrative which, unusually for the serial, takes place over one night and the following day.

One scene in the film is particularly interesting in terms of Swedish cinema and social attitudes. Apart from Widerberg and Bergman, the most successful Swedish film export in the 1960s and into the 1970s was the sex film (which features in a potentially criminal activity in Book 10). Sjöwall and Wahlöö write candidly and plainly about criminal acts that involve sexual assault and equally (though with more intimacy) about the very occasional moments when the detectives make love to their partners. The scene in the film, early in the morning in Kollberg's family home with his wife Gun and their toddler, perfectly captures the tone of the books. The scene is not intended to be titillating and it is not gratuitous – it simply and quickly establishes Kollberg's personality (and contrasts his good fortune with that of his friend Beck in his dismal marriage).

The book's title in English translates as *The Abominable Man from Säffle* (Säffle is a small town in Värmland, central Sweden). The man is sixty-year-old Chief Inspector Stig Nyman who, at the beginning of the story, is lying in a hospital bed when an assailant breaks into his room and brutally murders him with a bayonet. The 'abominable' tag comes from Kollberg who remembers Nyman first from his military training. Nyman's later rise in the police force represents many of the things wrong with government policies on policing. But Beck is still charged with finding out why Nyman died in this way. The book is structured in a familiar and almost cinematic way in three clear acts. In the first, the murder is committed, discovered and the investigation instigated. In the second, Rönn and Melander between them discover the brutal actions in Nyman's past and who might be the suspect. Beck is not idle in these first two acts. He manages and directs the team, interviews witnesses and makes interventions. The final third of the narrative then becomes a prolonged and exciting action sequence involving first Kollberg and Larsson and eventually Beck. They must stop the suspect, a former police marksman, from killing more officers from a vantage point on the rooftop of a high building in central Stockholm. *The Man on the Roof* is a title which does change the emphasis provided by the novel. Åke Eriksson, the shooter, is the symptom of the problem. Nyman was the problem.

The Man on the Roof *as a 'political film'*

Up until the first shot is fired, wounding a uniformed officer, Widerberg uses only 'direct sound'. Only as the action begins does a music score underpin the police 'chase'. The action itself follows the same model as the investigation and the three detectives strive to stop the shooter, using intelligence and making tactical decisions which do place the trio in danger but are not stupidly 'heroic'. The highlight is a sequence that requires Kollberg to rescue Beck in an awkward and nail-biting procedure with an emotional kick. At one point, Widerberg crashes a helicopter on to a Metro station, emphasising the dangers of a heavy-handed approach. The crowd scenes on the street are very convincing, as shot by the experienced documentary and TV cinematographer Odd-Geir Sæther and his younger partner Per Källberg.

The Man on the Roof illustrates the political message of Sjöwall and Wahlöö in two ways. First, the overall approach adopted by Widerberg means that we become engaged with the investigation of a crime through the characters of the detective team and the presentation of the impact of the events on the streets of Stockholm. We see that the detectives know their city and its inhabitants as well as the potential flaws in their own force. There are small human touches such as when a weary Rönn still has time to comfort a young uniformed officer who is overwhelmed by the savage attack on Nyman. This is not a 'crime story' that happens to take place in Stockholm; it is, as in the best neorealist films, a story that arises from the policing of the city and how it interacts with the lives of the citizens and individual police officers.

Second, the structure of the narrative presents two clear arguments. In the first, we learn about Stig Nyman's past behaviour in the military and the police. This is not a narrative about one rogue police officer. It is an indictment of recruitment and training practices, of institutionalised brutality and the kind of 'canteen culture' in which younger officers are 'schooled' in how to protect their superiors from internal investigation. The novel uses the 'Challenor Case' in the UK in the 1960s as a reference point for a notorious instance of corruption and cover-up. Challenor was an ex-World War II hero whose brutal actions as a Metropolitan Police detective sergeant were eventually challenged by a member of the National Council for Civil Liberties in 1963. Challenor punched a man after arresting him at a demonstration and then planted evidence on him. Challenor was sent to trial but found unfit to plead because of mental health issues. A subsequent inquiry was widely seen as a whitewash and the case became a public scandal. Operation Countryman finally tackled corruption in the Met in the late 1970s but was still not conclusive. Widerberg attempts to represent this argument distilled into confrontations between Beck and one of Nyman's 'loyal' colleagues, Sergeant Hult.

In the third act of the film, attention shifts to the mismanagement and politicisation of police action. In Sjöwall and Wahlöö's world, criminal activity and policing are both inextricably linked to changes in society. The media quickly become involved in the street scenes when one of the police hierarchy mistrusted by Beck, Superintendent Malm, tells a journalist his plans for an assault on the rooftop before he has even spoken to Beck. As a result, a military-style operation by specialist officers is ordered and this leads to several more police deaths. As if to make the point even clearer, the final action of the film sees a volunteer civilian marksman, recruited by Larsson, disable the gunman and end the crisis.

Ultimately, whilst *The Man on the Roof* does share elements with Hollywood crime thrillers of the period, not least the street footage of a film like *The French Connection* (1971), Beck and his team are used by Sjöwall, Wahlöö and Widerberg to make powerful statements about the politics of policing in Sweden, something that connects the film to the other European political thrillers discussed in this dossier.

References

Blomkvist, M. (2011). '"The Swedish Film Database": Bo Widerberg' (D. Jones, Trans.). Retrieved from: www.svenskfilmdatabas.se/en/
France, L. (2009, 22 November). 'The Queen of Crime'. *The Observer*. Retrieved from: www.theguardian.com/books/2009/nov/22/crime-thriller-maj-sjowall-sweden
Liukkonen, P. (2008). '"Authors Calendar": Sjöwall and Wahlöö'. Retrieved from: http://authorscalendar.info
Sjöwall, M. (2010). *Time Shift – Nordic Noir: The Story of Scandinavian Crime Fiction*. Bristol: BBC Productions.
Sjöwall, M. and Wahlöö, P. (2016). *The Abominable Man* (J. Tate, Trans.). London: 4th Estate. First published by P. A. Norstedt and Söners Forlag in 1971.
Soila, T., Widding, A. S. and Iverson, G. (1998). *Nordic National Cinemas*. London: Routledge.

17

The legacy of the 1970s European political thriller

Andy Willis

Figure 18 *New Order* (2020), courtesy of MUBI

This dossier has outlined the impact of some of the political thrillers produced in Europe in the 1970s. Of course, decades in this context are arbitrary boundaries created to help categorise the output of various film industries based in different countries across the continent. And equally, cycles of production such as this often began before the start of the decade and continue into the following historical period. The season that initiated this dossier reflects this, starting with Z released in 1969 and finishing with *Circle of Deceit* (*Die Fälschung*, Volker Schlöndorff), which arrived in cinemas towards the end of 1981. Whilst films such as the ones discussed in this dossier have had a significant cultural and industrial impact, one also finds that they have left a legacy that indicates they have continued to influence filmmakers long after their initial release. In this chapter, I will highlight some of the films and filmmakers that clearly show the influence of European political thrillers of the 1970s. This is variously through the way they construct their narratives, engage with contemporary and historical political situations and use well-known performers as a way of attracting audiences. In these ways, it is possible to identify how they operate in a tradition of making commercially orientated political cinema. These films exist across the world in a wide variety of contexts. Here, I offer a brief overview of some of the work that, for me, displays the influence and legacy of the European political thriller of the 1970s.

Some of those who continued to make political thrillers in the years after the 1970s were in fact some of the key practitioners of that decade who remained committed to the form. One director who still displayed a connection to the idea of the political thriller was Costa-Gavras. Following a successful decade working in Europe, Costa-Gavras began to work with companies that were based in the USA as well. The first product of this collaboration was *Missing* (1982), a thriller that follows the search, by his father and wife, for a missing American journalist in the aftermath of the overthrow of the Allende government in Chile. Revisiting the Latin American setting of *State of Siege (État de Siège*, 1972), *Missing* proved to be a significant success, winning the *Palme d'Or* at the 1982 Cannes Film Festival. Costa-Gavras followed this film with *Hanna K.* (1983), which deals with the Israel–Palestine conflict through the story of a Jewish lawyer assigned to defend a Palestinian accused of terrorism. *Hanna K.* was less of a success, and after that, Costa-Gavras continued to embrace the political thriller format to explore more directly American subjects. These included *Betrayed* (1988), which investigated the willingness of white supremacists to turn to terrorism; *Music Box* (1989), which focused on the trial and investigation of a Hungarian-American immigrant accused of being a war criminal; and *Mad City* (1997), which explored the psychological impact of unemployment. After *Mad City*, which was received poorly by critics, Costa-Gavras returned exclusively to filmmaking in Europe where, in 2002, he directed the more successful and once again controversial *Amen*, about the collaboration of the Vatican with the Nazis during World War II.

Whilst Costa-Gavras worked in both the USA and Europe following the 1970s, the political thriller remained a form to which filmmakers who wanted to address social issues within the French film industry returned. Two films that reflect this are *The Army of the Crime* (*L'Armée du crime*, 2009) and *Outside the Law* (*Hors-la-loi*, Rachid Bouchareb, 2010). The former, directed by Robert Guédiguian, explores the activities of the Manouchian Group who took part in the resistance to German occupation during World War II. They were the subject of a notorious poster which contained images of ten members who were executed in 1944 and described them as not liberators but an army of crime. Whilst not renowned for working in the thriller format as are a number of the directors explored in this dossier, Guédiguian has built a reputation as one of the most political filmmakers currently working in France, and so it is not surprising that when the material he is dealing suits it, he will work within the form. Similarly, Rachid Bouchareb, director of *Outside the Law*, is not a filmmaker usually associated with the form of the thriller. His films often explore issues relating to the experience of colonial subjects and the relationship between France and its colonies, in particular, Algeria. With *Outside the Law*, he works within a commercial style of cinema that evokes the conventions of the thriller format to tell the story of three brothers who are part of the Algerian liberation struggle. Both these works show that politically motivated directors still find aspects of the thriller useful as a method of engaging audiences in the political motivations and actions of their characters.

European television has also been a fruitful medium through which the political thriller has found new momentum in the twenty-first century, often by offering a variety of contemporary tales of conspiracy. Perhaps the most high-profile example has been the series of adaptations of Stieg Larsson's novels *The Girl with the Dragon Tattoo*, *The Girl Who Played with Fire*, and *The Girl Who Kicked the Hornets' Nest*, which, following cinema releases in Sweden during 2009, were extended into a six-part series and broadcast on Swedish television in 2010. The long-form format allowed for an extended exploration of conspiracies involving the state and other dangerous, anti-democratic operatives that picked up the mantel of the political thrillers of the 1970s. Its success led to political conspiracies being at the core of other European television series such as the Belgian *Salamander*. Broadcast in 2012 and 2013, with a follow-up series in 2018, *Salamander* involves labyrinthine investigations by Inspector Paul Gerardi into conspiracies by the country's elite, including politicians, industrialists, bankers and the judiciary, aimed at destabilising the country. Like the Larsson adaptations, *Salamander*, and other series such as the UK-produced *The Shadow Line* (2011) and *Black Earth Rising* (2018), suggest that the political thriller is easily adapted into formats suitable for television, and that, with the rise of streaming services, due to this, it can continue to be a vibrant and relevant medium through which to explore contemporary political issues as the twenty-first century progresses.

The legacy of the European political thriller is certainly present in Spanish filmmaking after the 1970s. As touched on earlier in this dossier, Spain after the death of General Franco in 1975 saw an increase in filmmakers using the form of the thriller to investigate political subjects. For example, Basque politics and the activities of separatist group ETA (*Euskadi Ta Askatasuna*) along with the Spanish state's attempts to counter them were, as Fraser Elliott has explored in his contribution on *Operación Ogro* (*Ogro*, 1979), something that was not really tackled in Spanish cinema until after the Franco regime had ended in 1975. As noted earlier, when José Luis Borau had tried to get an earlier version of what became *B Must Die!* (*Hay que matar a B.*, 1974) passed by the censor, he was told that its Basque Country setting was too politically sensitive a location. Things were significantly different during and after the transition to democracy in Spain, and filmmakers slowly began to address the political issues involved in the Basque region, with a number adopting the form of the political thriller.

Director Imanol Uribe began his exploration of Basque politics with the documentary *El proceso de Burgos* (*The Burgos Trial*, 1979). This focused on a military trial that was tasked with convicting ETA activists for actions that had been perpetrated in the previous years and which were to be considered as criminal acts. His first fiction feature to deal with the Basque struggle was *La fuga de Segovia* (*Escape from Segovia*, 1981) which told, through the memories of an exiled political prisoner, the story of an attempted escape by ETA members from the prison in Segovia. Uribe began to draw together Basque politics and genre conventions once again with the mystery-tinged *La Muerte de Mikel* (*The Death of Mikel*) released in 1984. With *Días contados* (*Running out of Time*, 1994), he mixed political characters and the criminal underworld in what is, of all his work up to then, most clearly defined as a thriller, albeit a thriller with a political setting rather than a political thriller in the mould of Costa-Gavras.

Yoyes (2000), directed by Helena Taberna, is an important example in this cycle of films focused on Basque politics. Unlike most of the other films that address these issues, it focuses on a female character, María Dolores González, an ETA activist known as Yoyes, and her attempt to leave the group and return to civilian life. The film is most often discussed as a drama or biopic rather than a thriller. However, there is certainly mileage in considering it alongside other works that create tension and jeopardy. The questions remain as the film progresses: will she be discovered and how will the information be released? The jeopardy offered by these issues creates tension, particularly the sequences following her return to Spain, her being used for pro-government propaganda and her being located and finally killed. As with other examples of the political thriller, such as *State of Siege* (1972), based on real events, this tension exists even though many in the audience are well aware of the ultimate outcome for the central character.

Described by critic Fionnuala Halligan as a 'cracking period political thriller' (2005), *The Wolf* (*El Lobo*, Miguel Courtois, 2004) was another work that clearly adopted the form of the political thriller, including chases, moments of high tension and a complex use of strategies of identification. *The Wolf*'s lineage was noted by Halligan, who states that it is 'the type of intelligent drama rarely seen these days – a throwback to Costa Gavras's *Z* or *Missing*' (2005). The film, as with so many political thrillers from Europe, tells a real-life story, here, of Mikel Lejarza, who in the early 1970s infiltrated ETA whilst working for the Spanish intelligence services. Driven by a muscular performance by Eduardo Noriega as Lejarza, one of the main departures from the model created by the likes of Costa-Gavras that marks *The Wolf* as different from some of the best-known examples from the 1970s, is that in creating a more historically set political thriller, it does not clearly position itself in relation to this politics. As Halligan notes, it offers 'a broad picture of both sides of the fence: Franco's corrupt military regime, the brutality of the terrorists, the tensions within ETA itself, and those caught in the middle' (2005). In doing so, it differs significantly from a number of the European political thrillers of the 1970s that were made by filmmakers who clearly were driven by a political commitment, most notably, on the left. The director of *The Wolf*, Miguel Courtois, would return to the Basque conflict with *GAL*. Released in 2006, and much more clearly critical of the operation of GAL (*Grupos Antiterroristas de Liberación*), the film follows two investigative journalists attempting to understand the activities of GAL and its death squads by tracking down its commander Ariza.

More recently, director Pablo Malo made *Lasa and Zabala* (*Lasa eta Zabala*, 2014), another film that engaged with the debates about the Spanish state's involvement in death squads, here, sent to France to neutralise ETA activists through the GAL initiative. When two bodies are discovered buried in quicklime near Alicante, two investigators determine to find out how they arrived there and ultimately if they could be Joxean Lasa and Joxi Zabala, who went missing in Bayonne in 1983. When director Malo visited HOME in 2015 to present his film at the ¡*Viva! Spanish and Latin American* festival, he discussed how he had drawn inspiration from films such as *Hidden Agenda* (Ken Loach, 1990) and *In the Name of the Father* (Jim Sheridan, 1993) that drew on the form of the political thriller to explore real-life incidents from the recent past. As Fionnuala Halligan noted in her review for *ScreenDaily*, like those films, *Lasa and Zabala* focuses 'on an investigation into the security services and resulting campaign for justice' (2014). In doing so, Malo manages to use a historical event to engage in political debates that are ongoing today, here, the issue of Basque nationalism and the state's response to it.

Outside the work that addresses the Basque issue, other Spanish filmmakers have also adopted the form of the political thriller. Interestingly, questions of definition raise their head regarding the films of Alberto Rodríguez, a Seville-based director who has worked extensively in the area of the political thriller. Discussing his works, Valeria Camporesi and Jara Fernández Meneses describe them as examples of the ' "quality thriller" as they share a "filmmaker-auteur" nature, good production values and an effort to obey the rules of the genre' (2018: 198), but they do not use the label political thriller beyond an occasional aside. However, when one looks at Rodríguez's work, in particular *Unit 7* (*Grupo 7*, 2012), *Marshland* (*La isla minima*, 2014) and *Smoke and Mirrors* (*El hombre de las mil caras*, 2016), the description of them as political thrillers in the mode of Costa-Gavras and Jorge Semprún seems most appropriate. Even though all three have historical settings, as Camporesi and Fernández Meneses insightfully note, whilst set in the recent past, these films also directly engage with the politics of the present:

> At the very moment when these three films were conceived and produced, a strong social and cultural movement (the Indignados) along with its subsequent political germinations (Podemos and its allies) were strongly questioning the way in which the story of the birth of democracy had been told until then in the public discourse, and began to piece together a new description of the roots and nature of the whole process.
>
> 2018: 199

Regarding *Marshland* in particular, director Rodríguez made a similar point, arguing:

> The historical context is essential. Marshland is a metaphor about the transition from Franco's dictatorship to democracy. A transition that was not well carried out, where many things were ignored. Looking again at the archives, we realised that at that time Spain had the same problems that we worry about today. The headlines were all about the debate of territoriality, the abortion law, the economic crisis, the general feeling of tension … That's why the 80s seemed to us to be a good backdrop.
>
> Evans, no date

As is shown by this recent crop of Spanish political thrillers, whilst for some directors the ambitions are the same as those making films in the 1970s, that is, to make political points in a manner that has the potential to engage audiences due to the commercial form adopted, for others, it is the commercial potential of the form of the thriller that has attracted them rather than the opportunity to present a particular political perspective on events portrayed.

The political thriller has also offered significant opportunities of making films that engaged with the politics of the day within the cinemas of Latin America. However, whilst there were examples of films that utilise the conventions of the form, such as *Operación Masacre* (*Operation Massacre*, Jorge Cedrón, 1973), which deals with the unsuccessful 1956 Peronist uprising in Argentina, the rise of authoritarian regimes across the continent meant that the construction of a popular political cinema became more difficult.

Once countries began to emerge from the oppression of the various military dictatorships that had taken control in the 1970s, Latin American filmmakers began to explore the opportunities offered by the political thriller. For example, in Argentina, the second decade of the twenty-first century produced some of the best examples of the form, many of which dealt with the memory and legacy of the dictatorship. *The Secret in Their Eyes* (*El secreto de sus ojos*, Juan José Campanella, 2009) moves between historical moments when two characters meet again after having first come together twenty-five years earlier as they investigated a brutal rape and murder. Through flashbacks, the suggestion is that the investigation was flawed due to the political context of the time. *Pasaje de vida* (*Passage of Life*, Diego Corsini, 2015) uses a similar device of shifting historical settings to also explore memory and trauma. Here, in contemporary Spain, an old man suffers from dementia whilst his son investigates what in his past might be upsetting him so much. In doing so, he discovers his father's past as a radical activist involved in acts of terrorism. Director Pablo Trapero also uses the political thriller to revisit Argentina's past with *The Clan* (*El Clan*, 2015). Here, the focus is on the Pucchio family, who, under the military dictatorship, kidnapped for extortion between 1982 and 1985. The brutality of the family is presented as shockingly everyday, revealing how for some, such acts were no longer seen as beyond the pale. The lead actor of *The Secret in Their Eyes*, Ricardo Darín, also plays the main role of Sosa in an earlier Trapero thriller, *Carancho* (*The Vulture*, 2010). He is an ambulance-chasing lawyer who lost his registration and is now working in the murkier end of medical insurance. As the film reveals the corrupt actions of Sosa's bosses, Trapero and his screenwriters use the thriller format for political ends as their story reveals the inadequacy of the medical and legal systems and the corruption that is endemic within their relationship.

Chilean filmmakers have also addressed the politics of the recent past. The 2020 feature *Matar a Pinochet* (*Kill Pinochet*, 2020) is an interesting example of a political thriller that takes the form, focusing on a real political event, yet manages to dilute the ideological drive behind the actions of its central characters, in this case, the left-wing plotters. The film tells the story of a real plot to kill Pinochet that was undertaken by the Manuel Rodríguez Patriotic

Front (FPMR), the armed wing of the Chilean Communist Party, on 7 September 1986. The filmmakers focus on an act of resistance to right-wing regimes, offering it as the simple act of righteousness without fully exploring the political position of those behind it. Ultimately, like a number of the films that embrace the form of the political thriller in the twenty-first century, it offers a range of thrills but in the final analysis seems strangely low on politics, which is even more striking given the Latin American context. An FPMR fighter and the plot to kill Pinochet are also central to the 2020 feature *My Tender Matador* (*Tengo Miedo Torero*, 2020) directed by Rodrigo Sepúlveda. Adapted from a novel by artist Pedro Lemebel, here, the fighter is in love with a transvestite, and the film explores the issue of the inclusion of gay sexuality in revolutionary politics. This is highlighted when the middle-aged transvestite says to the young revolutionary 'If there's ever a revolution that includes us, let me know. I'll be there, front row.' The discussion of freedom in this instance takes a historical story and utilises it to discuss a set of still very contemporary issues. Because of this, whilst it is not a political thriller, Sepúlveda's use of the historical backdrop of revolutionary politics has more resonance than those films that use historic and political events as almost a mere setting for cinematic action and thrills.

Described by John Hopewell as a 'near-future dystopia thriller' that 'is a withering, brutal and discomfiting portrait of Mexico's heartless and corruption-sodden stinking rich' (2020), *New Order* (*Nuevo Orden*, Michel Franco, 2020) is one of the most interesting recent explorations of contemporary politics that utilises narrative aspects associated with the political thriller. Michel Franco's Mexican-set film opens during a high-society wedding as social unrest erupts in the streets outside the compound where events are taking place. The confusion caused by the protests is initially shown as cover for a gang to rob the guests, then as an opportunity for a renegade military group to kidnap people, including the bride who has left the compound, for ransom. The wider protests ultimately lead to the establishment of military rule. As with the political thrillers of the 1970s, street protests and the collapse of law and order reflect a strategy of tension that ultimately sees a coup d'etat. Whilst the film is a co-production with France, the director's stated ambitions were to make something that spoke to the specificity of

Mexican society whilst also acknowledging that the core issues were more universal. Speaking to *Variety*, he observed that 'Mexico's upper class are asking for trouble: They're building up to a situation that will finally explode … Upper-class behavior will build until a day when everything breaks down' (Hopewell, 2020), and in an interview with Screen Daily, Franco stated that the film also:

> Came out of my concerns regarding social disparity, not only in Mexico but worldwide … Throughout writing this movie – the process started five, six years ago – we've seen the Yellow Vests in France, and civil disorder in Chile, Colombia, Hong Kong, and now Black Lives Matter. So it's either social disparity or racial problems or a combination, and instead of finding real answers, the response everywhere is totalitarian governments trying to get back to what they call normal. But we shouldn't accept the way things are as normal and to me it's a time bomb that's going to explode in our face sooner rather than later.
>
> Kay, 2020

What is striking when one considers the legacy of the 1970s European political thrillers is the flexibility of the format. This allows filmmakers to use it to explore the past as much as it does the contemporary. What stands out about this is the fact that certain of those utilising the thriller form choose to almost de-politicise it whilst others use it to directly address the most urgent socio-political issues of the day. This without doubt suggests that as the twenty-first century progresses in a turbulent and increasingly polarised fashion, the political thriller will continue to offer filmmakers an approach that is potentially attractive to audiences and can introduce some challenging and progressive perspectives on the modern world.

References

Camporesi, V. and Fernández Meneses, J. (2018). 'Making Sense of Genre: The "Quality Thriller" as a Vehicle to Revise a Controversial Past in Recent Spanish Cinema'. *Studies in European Cinema*, 15 (2–3), 198–214.

Evans, A. (no date). 'Dark Soul – Interview with Spanish Film Director Alberto Rodriguez'. *Latino Life*. Retrieved from: www.latinolife.co.uk/articles/dark-soul-interview-spanish-film-director-alberto-rodriguez

Halligan, F. (2005). 'The Wolf (El Lobo)'. *ScreenDaily*. Retrieved from: www.screendaily.com/the-wolf-el-lobo/4022905.article
Halligan, F. (2014). '*Lasa and Zabala*'. *ScreenDaily*. Retrieved from: www.screendaily.com/lasa-and-zabala/5078164.article
Hopewell, J. (2020, 9 September). '*New Order*: Director Michel Franco on Social Cataclysm in Mexico'. *Variety*. Retrieved from: https://variety.com/2020/film/festivals/michel-franco-venice-competition-new-order-social-cataclysm-1234764297/
Kay, J. (2020, 7 September). '*New Order* Director Michel Franco on the Time Bomb That Is Waiting to Explode'. *ScreenDaily*. Retrieved from: www.screendaily.com/features/new-order-director-michel-franco-on-the-time-bomb-that-is-waiting-to-explode/5152892.article
Rivera, A. (2016). 'Alberto Rodríguez Director: "Every Film Is a World of Its Own"', *Cineuropa*. Retrieved from: https://cineuropa.org/en/interview/315354/

18

The season: Films screened as part of *States of Danger and Deceit*

Rachel Hayward, Ellen Smith and Andy Willis

In the winter of 2017, HOME presented a season of nail-biting thrillers that expose the political tensions that reverberated across Europe in the 1970s. A decade when the social turmoil that marked the late 1960s gave way to a more strident politics that involved stark and sometimes violent contrasts between left and right. A decade that was scarred by the emergence of uncompromisingly radical groups such as the Red Army Faction and the Red Brigades. In response to this charged moment, a number of filmmakers across Europe turned to the format of the thriller. Stylish and enduringly popular with audiences, they saw it as the perfect vehicle through which to explore conspiracies, authoritarian regimes and political violence.

Beginning with Costa-Gavras's legendary *Z* (1969), *States of Danger and Deceit: European Political Thrillers in the 1970s* offered audiences the chance to discover or revisit some of the decade's key works including *Investigation of a Citizen above Suspicion* (1970), *The Lost Honour of Katharina Blum* (1975) and *Illustrious Corpses* (1976), films that still influence the way in which politically engaged filmmakers approach their work and engage with popular forms and genres.

Programme curated by Andy Willis, Professor of Film Studies at the University of Salford and Senior Visiting Curator: Film at HOME, produced by Rachel Hayward, HOME's Head of Film Strategy, and coordinated by Jessie Gibbs, HOME Film Team. Presented with the support of the BFI, awarding funds from the National Lottery.

Figure 19 Season brochure cover, courtesy of HOME, Manchester

Circle of Deceit (Die Fälschung)

Director Volker Schlöndorff/West Germany/France 1981/108 minutes/German and French with English subtitles

Bruno Ganz, Hanna Schygulla, Jean Carmet

In *Circle of Deceit*, Schlöndorff deftly mixes the personal and the political to great effect in a film that stars two of the biggest names of the New German Cinema, Bruno Ganz and Hanna Schygulla. Shot on location, the film drips authenticity in its creation of a dizzyingly complex world within which Ganz plays an experienced 'seen-it-all' journalist who has to face up to a series of moral questions when he arrives in Beirut to report on a political situation that is lurching into war.

The Deputy (El diputado)

Director Eloy de la Iglesia/Spain 1978/110 minutes/Spanish with English subtitles

José Sacristán, María Luisa San José, José Luis Alonso

During Spain's transition to democracy following the death of General Franco, a communist politician is elected to parliament. As the country opens up to new ideas, he slowly comes to terms with his own sexuality, embarking upon an affair with a juvenile delinquent. He realises that his actions expose him to manipulation from the extreme right-wing forces still loyal to the ideals of the dictatorship and who will go to any lengths to resist democracy.

The Day of the Jackal

Director Fred Zinnemann/Great Britain, France 1973/143 minutes

Edward Fox, Terence Alexander, Michel Auclair

A UK–France co-production, Fred Zinnemann's legendary film explores the attempts of a right-wing paramilitary group to assassinate

French President General De Gaulle following the independence of Algeria. Boasting a career-defining performance from Edward Fox and replete with many political twists and turns, *The Day of the Jackal* is one of the best thrillers of the 1970s.

Days of '36 (Meres tou '36)

Director Theodoros Angelopoulos/Greece 1972/104 minutes/Greek with English subtitles

Vangelis Kazan, Kostas Pavlou, Thanos Grammenos

During the 1970s, Angelopoulos made films that were formally challenging and highly stylised. On occasion, these used the narrative conventions of the political thriller to a very different effect to the slick films that make up the majority of this season. In *Days of '36*, an imprisoned murderer takes a government official hostage in prison, sparking a political crisis. Full of Angelopoulos's trademark symmetrical compositions, this reads like a thriller but through the director's use of film form resists the normal pleasures of the genre.

Don't Torture a Duckling (Non si sevizia un paperino)

Director Lucio Fulci/Italy 1972/102 minutes/Italian with English subtitles

Florinda Bolkan, Barbara Bouchet, Tomas Milian

A great example of the ways in which a popular form, here the *giallo* style of violent thriller, can be used to critique society's institutions. Set in rural Italy, Lucio Fulci's film focuses on a series of brutal murders where the killer seems to target young boys on the verge of adulthood. As the media flocks to the village where the victims lived, suspicion falls on those residents who, due to their lifestyles, are considered outsiders. Rumour has it that Fulci was subsequently blacklisted due to his critical representation of Italy's powerful social institutions.

The Flight (Die Flucht)

Director Roland Gräf/East Germany 1977/94 minutes/German with English subtitles

Armin Mueller-Stahl, Jenny Gröllmann, Erika Pelikowsky

The final film made by the great German actor Armin Mueller-Stahl in the East – he would later memorably link up with Costa-Gavras in the US for *Music Box* (1989). In *The Flight*, he plays a doctor who when dutifully following procedure and applying to travel outside the German Democratic Republic (GDR) to attend a conference is refused permission. Dismayed by the state bureaucracy, he becomes involved with an underground network who promise they can get him out of the country. Given it was made in the East, all does not go to plan.

Illustrious Corpses (Cadaveri eccellenti)

Director Francesco Rosi/Italy, France 1976/120 minutes/Italian with English subtitles

Lino Ventura, Tino Carraro, Marcel Bozzuffi

In an Italy rife with mistrust and paranoia, judges are being murdered. Lino Ventura's quietly effective detective is appointed to investigate who is responsible and soon begins to unearth an array of corruption and duplicity within the corridors of power. Highly atmospheric, this is perhaps the archetypal political film of the 1970s and displays to great effect Rosi's brilliant visual style.

Investigation of a Citizen above Suspicion (Indagine su un cittadino al di sopra di ogni sospetto)

Director Elio Petri /Italy 1970/115 minutes/Italian with English subtitles

Gian Maria Volonté, Florinda Bolkan, Gianni Santuccio

In Elio Petri's visually stunning and beautifully composed film, a corrupt police official decides to show how untouchable he is by creating a murder scene where the evidence can only lead investigators to him. Starring the iconic left-wing actor Gian Maria Volonté, who provides a mesmerising performance, this is a sly and slick condemnation of the state and the police from one of Italy's major political filmmakers of the 1960s and 1970s.

Killer Cop (La polizia ha le mani legate)

Director Luciano Ercoli/Italy 1975/97 minutes/Italian with English subtitles

Claudio Cassinelli, Arthur Kennedy, Franco Fabrizi

In this Milan-set, low-budget gem, director Luciano Ercoli creates a political thriller full of 1970s Italian style. After a terrorist bomb explodes in a busy hotel, the official investigation gets caught up in politics and bureaucracy. As the bombers go on the run, the only hope of catching them lies with Cassenelli's determined narcotics cop, who accidently got caught in the mayhem. This highly effective *Poliziotteschi* shows how the radical politics of the decade bled into genre filmmaking in Italy.

Knife in the Head (Messer im Kopf)

Director Reinhard Hauff/West Germany 1978/108 minutes/German with English subtitles

Bruno Ganz, Angela Winkler, Hans Christian Blech

Shot in the head whilst seemingly innocently visiting his wife at a youth centre and left paralysed, Hoffman (Bruno Ganz) finds himself caught in between the police and terrorists as he tries to piece together his memories of the event rather than accepting the various versions told by others who wish to exploit his injury for their own ends. Driven by a superlative performance by Ganz, Hauff's film reflects the paranoia and political tension within West Germany as the 1970s drew to a close.

The Long Good Friday

Director John Mackenzie/Great Britain 1980/115 minutes/English

Bob Hoskins, Helen Mirren, Paul Freeman

In this landmark British thriller, gangster Harold Shand, memorably played with great relish by Bob Hoskins, dreams of developing London's rundown dockland and becoming a legitimate businessman. He also wants a partnership with the American Mafia. However, his plans are put in jeopardy when a number of his associates are attacked. Increasingly paranoid, Harold sets out to discover who is behind them and slowly realises the answer is much more political than he ever imagined.

The Lost Honour of Katharina Blum
(Die verlorene Ehre der Katharina Blum)

Directors Volker Schlöndorff, Margarethe von Trotta/West Germany 1975/106 minutes/German with English subtitles

Angela Winkler, Mario Adorf, Dieter Laser

A key political film of the New German Cinema, Volker Schlöndorff and Margarethe von Trotta co-directed and adapted *The Lost Honour of Katharina Blum* from the controversial novel by Heinrich Böll. Set in a climate of fear and paranoia, Angela Winkler plays the young woman of the title whose life is slowly destroyed by the media following her meeting a young man who is suspected by the authorities of being a political activist.

Man on the Roof (Mannen på taket)

Director Bo Widerberg/Sweden 1976/110 minutes/Swedish with English subtitles

Carl-Gustaf Lindstedt, Sven Wollter, Thomas Hellberg

Adapted from the Martin Beck novel *The Abominable Man* by legendary left-leaning Swedish crime writers Maj Sjöwall and Per

Wahlöö, *The Man on the Roof* is a great example of a 1970s Scandi-crime film. Here, Beck, played by Carl-Gustaf Lindstedt, and his team investigate a brutal murder in a hospital, encountering stories of police brutality as they progress, which in turn leads to a thrilling climax on the rooftops of Stockholm.

The Mattei Affair (Il caso Mattei)

Director Francesco Rosi /Italy 1972/116 minutes/Italian and English with partial English subtitles

Gian Maria Volonté, Luigi Squarzina, Peter Baldwin

A key title in the development of Francesco Rosi's style of investigative thriller, *The Mattei Affair* focuses on the death of Enrico Mattei, an influential businessman who made enemies in the mafia. His story is interspersed with Rosi's investigation into the disappearance of his friend, journalist Mauro De Mauro, who was undertaking research for the film. Again driven by a thoughtful performance from Gian Maria Volonté, *The Mattei Affair* is one of Rosi's finest works.

Operación Ogro (Ogro)

Director Gillo Pontecorvo /Spain, Italy 1979/115 minutes/Italian with English subtitles

Gian Maria Volonté, Ángela Molina, Saverio Marconi

From the director of *Battle of Algiers* and starring Gian Maria Volonté alongside Eusebio Poncela, José Sacristán and Ángela Molina. This story of the assassination by ETA of Colonel Carrero Blanco, Spanish dictator Franco's right-hand man, comes with heavyweight credentials. Less well known than Pontecorvo's 1966 classic, this is a taut thriller that offers a complex set of positions in relation to what some called an act of terror and others political resistance.

Seven Days in January (Siete días de enero)

Director Juan Antonio Bardem/Spain, France 1979/124 minutes/Spanish with English subtitles

Manuel Ángel Egea, Fernando Sánchez Polack

Following the end of the Franco dictatorship in Spain, a rightwing hit squad targets the offices of a group of left-wing labour lawyers on Calle Atocha in Madrid. Will their actions destabilise the state and bring about the political change they desire? Based on a notorious series of real events and directed with careful precision by Juan Antonio Bardem, long an oppositional filmmaker in Spain, this is a key cultural work of the country's transition to democracy and reflects the political uncertainty of the era.

Special Section (Section spéciale)

Director Costa-Gavras /France, Italy, West Germany 1975/118 minutes/French and German with English subtitles

Louis Seigner, Roland Bertin, Michael Lonsdale

With *Special Section*, director Costa-Gavras turned his attention to events in France during World War II. When a German officer is killed, the Nazi occupying forces demand swift action in punishing the culprits. To appease them, a special court is created, presided over by a group of ambitious and subservient judges, with the aim of convicting a group of six men coldly used as scapegoats. Costa-Gavras was awarded Best Director at the 1975 Cannes Film Festival for *Special Section*.

State of Siege (État de siège)

Director Costa-Gavras/France, Italy 1972/120 minutes/French with English subtitles

Yves Montand, Renato Salvatori, O. E. Hasse

Written by Franco Solinas (*The Battle of Algiers*), *State of Siege* is perhaps the greatest political thriller of the 1970s. Costa-Gavras once again calls on Yves Montand to lead this story of an American, supposedly only working as an agricultural advisor regarding international development, who is kidnapped by guerrillas in Uruguay. The taut story is told against the backdrop of repressive politics, death squads and American involvement in Latin America.

Twilight's Last Gleaming

Director Robert Aldrich/West Germany, United States 1977/144 minutes/English

Burt Lancaster, Richard Widmark, Roscoe Lee Browne

A West German–US co-production shot mainly at the Bavaria film studios, this neglected work is one of Robert Aldrich's best films. It is driven by a wonderful performance from Burt Lancaster who plays a renegade US general disillusioned by his country's involvement in Vietnam and aware of a top-secret document that acknowledged the war could not be won. To try and make the powers that be reveal the document to the public, he hijacks a nuclear silo and threatens to launch a series of bombs. Utilising split screens to great effect, this is a taut political thriller of the highest order.

Z

Director Costa-Gavras/France 1969/127 minutes/French with English subtitles

Yves Montand, Irene Papas, Jean-Louis Trintignant

Winner of the Oscar for Best Foreign Language Film in 1970, after also having been nominated for Best Picture, Z remains one of the most influential political thrillers of all time. Jean-Louis Trintignant plays a magistrate assigned to investigate the supposed accidental death of a left-wing politician, memorably played by Yves Montand. In the course of his work, he uncovers a series of deceits and lies that attempt to hide the real political motivation of the killing.

Contextualising events

As well as the films in the season, HOME hosted a number of events aimed at developing audience engagement with its themes and content. These included the following.

One-hour intro/Political thrillers in the 1970s: From *Z* to *Circle of Deceit*

Politically, the 1970s was a turbulent decade and many filmmakers, writers and actors felt driven to explore some of its most pressing issues on screen. One of the results was a memorable cycle of politically motivated thrillers that attempted to bring the charged atmosphere of the streets on to cinema screens across Europe. Through an exploration of some of the key works and practitioners present in *States of Danger and Deceit*, this one-hour intro helped contextualise the season.

One-hour intro/Beck and the roots of Nordic Noir

Maj Sjöwall and Per Wahlöö's ten crime novels from the 1960s and 1970s featuring Inspector Martin Beck have had a major impact on Swedish – and international – film and TV. Their importance lies partly in their critical commentary on Swedish society, which in turn inspired Henning Mankell and other more recent crime narratives from Nordic countries. This introductory talk explored the Beck legacy and the distinctiveness of 'Nordic Noir' films and TV series.

One-hour intro/Looking at the career of Bruno Ganz

This one-hour intro focused on the work of the Swiss-German actor who, at the age of seventy-five, can look back on a long and varied career both in theatre and cinema. He has not shied away from difficult and controversial work, which makes him very interesting to explore. The talk was accompanied by film clips illustrating the versatility of this charismatic actor.

Debate: The space and place of women in the political thriller

This discussion focused on the place made available for women in the political thrillers of the 1970s. Given the strong presence of women in a number of radical organisations of the decade, was similar space made available for their representation on screen? Reference was made to a number of films screened during *States of Danger and Deceit* but also to other works of the period.

Event/The legacy of the 1970s political thriller

To discuss the politics of utilising the format of the thriller and the legacy of the work contained in *States of Danger and Deceit*, curator Andy Willis was joined by Berlin-based artist Declan Clarke, whose film-based work is greatly informed by both the politics of the 1970s and the aesthetic forms adopted within the films in the season.

Index

Aldrich, Robert 15, 187
Amen (2002) 68
Angelopoulos, Theo ix, 2, 120, 121, 148, 149, 150, 151, 152, 153, 154, 155, 156, 181
Army of the Crime, The (*L'Armée du crime*, 2009) 169
Austin, Guy 28

Bardem, Juan Antonio 123, 124, 186
Barka, Ben 49, 51, 52, 53, 57, 58
Barzman, Ben 24, 49, 55, 56, 58
Barzman, Norma 23, 55, 56, 57, 58
Battle of Algiers, The (*La battaglia di Algeri*, 1966) 35, 44, 51, 58, 121, 131, 186
Bergfelder, Tim 100
Berry, John 23, 26, 56
Betrayed (1988) 38, 168
Biskind, Peter 46, 47
Blair, Betsy 23, 123
Boisset, Yves 8, 24, 49, 52, 53, 54, 58
Böll, Heinrich 104, 110, 111, 115, 117, 184
Bondanella, Peter 34, 71, 81, 82, 99
Borau, José Louis 122, 123, 170

Bouchareb, Rachid 169
Brechtian aesthetics 148, 149
Brigate Rosse (*Red Brigades*) 75, 94, 132
Bullet for the General Bullet for the General (*Quién sabe?*, 1966) 13, 45, 73, 80, 130
Burn! (*Queimada*, 1969) 44, 130, 131

Cahiers du Cinema 8, 23
Canby, Vincent 38, 65, 69
Cannes Film Festival 59, 66, 70, 78, 162, 168, 186
Carné, Marcel 22
Case Is Closed, Forget It, The 14
Cayatte, André 22, 29
Chabrol, Claude 27, 29
Cineaste (magazine) 18, 25, 26, 37, 38, 40, 41, 44, 47, 48, 82, 91, 135
Cipriani, Stelvio 97
Circle of Deceit (*Die Fälschung*, 1981) 167, 180, 188
Cohn-Bendit, Daniel 8
Communist Party of Italy (PCI) 72
Comolli, Jean-Luc and Paul Narboni 8
Con uñas y dientes (*Tooth and Nail*, 1978) 125
Confession, The (*L'aveu*, 1970) 31, 36, 37, 39, 49, 59

Index

Confessions of a Police Commisioner (*Confessione di un commissario di polizia al procuratore della repubblica*, 1971) 14
Costa-Gavras 2, 8, 12, 15, 21, 25, 29, 30, 31, 32, 33, 34, 35, 36, 37, 38, 39, 40, 41, 42, 43, 44, 46, 47, 48, 49, 51, 53, 54, 56, 58, 59, 60, 61, 62, 63, 64, 65, 66, 67, 68, 69, 70, 78, 107, 120, 123, 168, 171, 173, 178, 182, 186, 187
Cowie, Peter 35, 38, 40, 47

Damiani, Damiano 13, 14, 45, 76, 77, 80, 81, 130
Dassin, Jules 23, 24, 56
Day of the Jackal (1973) 15, 101, 180, 181
Day of the Owl 13, 77, 80, 81
Days of '36 (*Meres tou '36*, 1972) 2, 12, 120, 121, 148, 150, 152, 153, 154, 155, 156, 181
de la Iglesia, Eloy 124, 126, 180
Dead Pigeon on Beethoven Street (*Tote Taube in der Beethovenstraße*, 1972) 14, 102, 103, 104
DEFA 11, 121, 136, 138, 146, 147
Delon, Alain 24, 34
Deputy, The (*El diputado*, 1978) 125, 180
Die Flucht (*The Flight*, 1977) 1, 11, 106, 121, 136, 140, 141, 143, 145, 146, 147, 182
Don't Torture a Duckling (1972) 8, 16, 71, 81, 181
Dziga Vertov Collective 8

Ebert, Roger 22, 35, 38
El proceso de Burgos (*The Burgos Trial*, 1979) 170
ETA (Euskadi Ta Askatasuna/ Basque Homeland and Liberty) 121, 127, 128, 170, 171, 172, 185

Fassbinder, Rainer Werner 101, 102, 105, 113, 140, 146
filone 71, 73, 76, 81, 95, 97, 98
Fisher, Austin 35, 48, 76, 81, 97, 99
Franchina, Basilio 49, 56
Fuller, Sam 14, 102, 103, 107

German Democratic Republic (GDR) 106, 107, 121, 136, 137, 138, 139, 140, 141, 143, 144, 145, 146, 182
giallo 16, 77, 80, 87, 181
Godard, Jean-Luc 8, 11, 12, 20, 28, 54
Gräf, Roland 121, 141
Guédiguian, Robert 169
Guerra, Tonino 77, 78

Hands over the City (*Le mani sulla città*, 1963) 12
Hanna K. (1983) 168
Hayward, Susan 20, 22, 63
Hennebelle, Guy 20, 21, 26, 29
Hill, John 8, 31
HOME 1, 179
Hopewell, John 30, 123, 124, 125, 126, 175, 177
House Un-American Activities Committee (HUAC) 23, 55
How to Kill a Judge (*Perché si uccide un magistrato*, 1975) 14, 80

Illustrious Corpses (*Cadaveri Eccellenti*, 1976) 4, 6, 13, 15, 77, 78, 79, 81, 124, 178, 182
Independent Cinema Office (ICO) 15, 37, 113, 117
Investigation of a Citizen Above Suspicion (1970) 1, 6, 8, 13, 18, 73, 75, 83, 85, 86, 87, 88, 89, 90, 91, 129, 178, 182
Italian Westerns 45

Joe Hill (1971) 119, 162

Kapò (1960) 44
Killer Cop (*La polizia ha le mani legate*, 1975) 8, 17, 76, 92, 93, 94, 95, 96, 97, 98, 183
Knife in the Head (*Messer im Kopf*, 1978) 8, 100, 102, 105, 108, 132, 183

L'Attentat (*Plot*, 1972) 2, 8, 49, 50, 51, 52, 53, 54, 55, 56, 57, 58
La Chinoise (1967) 11
Larsson, Stieg 157, 169
Lasa and Zabala (*Lasa eta Zabala*, 2014) 172
Lipman, Jerzy 103
Lizzani, Carlo 73, 82
London, Artur 36, 37
Long Good Friday, The (1980) 119, 120, 184
Losey, Joseph 24, 26, 55, 56, 62
Lucky Luciano (1974) 13, 78, 79, 129

Main d'oeuvre immigré (MOI) 32
Malo, Pablo 172
Man on the Roof (*Mannen på taket*, 1976) 5, 12, 15, 119, 157, 159, 161, 163, 164, 165, 184, 185
Manchurian Candidate, The (1962) 5
Mann, Anthony 56
Matar a Pinochet (*Kill Pinochet*, 2020) 174
Mattei Affair, The (*Il Caso Mattei*, 1972) 13, 78, 79, 129, 185
May '68 5, 8, 19, 20, 22, 28, 33, 57
Michalczyk, John J. 25, 28, 33, 44, 46, 48, 66, 69
mise en scène 34, 65, 107, 149
Missing (1982) 38, 168
Mitrione, Dan A. 39, 40
Möller, Olaf 52, 58
Montand, Yves 23, 25, 30, 31, 33, 34, 40, 41, 42, 44, 56, 67, 186, 187
Moro, Aldo 75, 85, 94, 132
Mueller-Stahl, Armin 121, 182

Nada (1974) 27, 28
Nero, Franco 13, 77
New Order (*Nuevo Orden*, 2020) 175
Nordic Noir 157, 158, 166, 188

Operación Ogro (1979) 9, 121, 127, 128, 129, 130, 131, 132, 134, 170, 185
Ophüls, Marcel 64, 70
Outside the Law (*Hors-la-loi*, 2010) 169
Outsider, The (1980) 14

Pakula, Alan J. 7, 8, 116
Palme, Olaf 161
Pasaje de vida (*Passage of Life*, 2015) 174
Pasolini, Pier Paolo 72, 74
Perrin, Jacques 56, 62, 66, 67
Petersen, Wolfgang 103, 115
Petley, Julian 24, 44, 48
Petri, Elio 8, 9, 13, 72, 77, 83, 88, 90, 91, 97, 120, 129, 182
Piazza Fontana bombing 75, 88, 93, 94
Piccoli, Michel 34, 53, 54
poliziottesco 76, 95, 96, 98
Pontecorvo, Gillo 22, 44, 51, 121, 127, 128, 130, 131, 132, 134, 135, 185
Popular Front (France) 22
Prague Spring 6, 37, 137
Prime, Rebecca 23, 55

Red Army Faction/Baader-Meinhof Group 3, 102, 139
Resnais, Alain 33, 112
Rififi (1955) 24
Rodríguez, Alberto 172, 177
Rosi, Francesco 8, 12, 22, 44, 77, 78, 81, 82, 97, 124, 129, 182, 185
Ryan, Michael and Douglas Kellner 6

Index

Salamander (2012–2018) 169, 170
Salvatore Giuliano (1962) 12, 44, 78
Scheider, Roy 53, 54
Schlöndorff, Volker 101, 104, 106, 110, 111, 112, 113, 114, 115, 132, 180, 184
Sciascia, Leonardo 13, 77, 78, 80, 81
Seberg, Jean 34, 53, 54
Secret in Their Eyes, The (El secreto de sus ojos, 2009) 174
Semprún, Jorge 25, 30, 32, 33, 36, 37, 38, 49, 54, 56, 57, 59, 61, 62, 63, 65, 66, 67, 68, 173
Seven Days in January (Siete días de enero, 1979) 124
Seven Days in May (1964) 5
Shocktroops (1 homme de trop, 1967) 32
Signoret, Simone 23, 31, 34, 56
Sjöwall, Maj and Per Wahlöö 119, 158, 159, 163, 166, 185, 188
Sleeping Car Murders, The (Compartiment tueurs, 1965) 31, 32, 33
Solinas, Franco 25, 40, 41, 44, 45, 46, 48, 61, 186
Spanish Communist Party (PCE) 32, 33, 123
Special Section (Section spéciale, 1975) 8, 12, 25, 31, 38, 59, 60, 61, 62, 63, 64, 65, 66, 67, 68, 69, 70, 186
State of Siege (État de Siège, 1972) 7, 8, 12, 25, 30, 37, 38, 39, 40, 41, 42, 43, 44, 45, 46, 47, 48, 59, 168, 171, 186
States of Danger and Deceit (UK tour) 17
Straub, Jean-Marie 21, 89, 116

Taberna, Helena 171
Tatort (1970 onwards) 14, 102, 103, 104, 107
Taubin, Amy 110, 113, 114, 116, 117
Tavernier, Bertrand 25, 26
Testi, Fabio 27
Time Out 27, 105, 107
Todo modo (1976) 13, 73, 77
Tout va bien (1972) 12
Trapero, Pablo 174
Trintignant, Jean-Louis 34, 53, 54, 57, 187
Tupamaros 38, 39, 40, 41, 45, 46, 47
Twilight's Last Gleaming (1977) 15, 187

Uribe, Imanol 170

Ventura, Lino 34, 79, 182
Vichy regime 60, 61, 62, 63, 64, 67, 68, 69
Visible Secrets
  Hong Kong's women filmmakers 5
Volonté, Gian Maria 8, 34, 53, 54, 73, 78, 79, 84, 85, 86, 122, 182, 183, 185
Von Trotta, Margarethe 94, 113

War Is Over, The (La guerre est finie, 1966) 33
Wayne, Mike 7, 31
We Still Kill the Old Way (A ciascuno il suo, 1967) 13, 73
Wicking, Christopher 6, 18
Widerberg, Bo 119, 161, 162, 163, 164, 165, 166, 184
Williams, Linda Ruth 6
Winkler, Angela 16, 111, 113, 114, 183, 184
Wolf, The (El Lobo, 2004) 171
Wood, Mary P. 71, 98
Working Class Goes to Heaven, The (La classe operaia va in paradiso, 1971) 13, 73

Years of lead 74, 75

Z (1969) 6, 12, 19, 30, 31, 51, 59, 64, 178